SEVEN DOORS IN

"Beth's book *Seven Doors In* is the story of a courageous woman who just does it! Gets it done, without excuses, overcoming obstacles. It's about how one woman's integrity and determination was so much larger than its aura that it spilled off and shone on the people she taught in such a way that changed their lives. It's proof that with nurturing—and lovingly giving of what you've been given to serve as God intended—miracles can happen! And miracles do happen. Sometimes saints come in the shape of a Beth!"

—KEITH DAVID
Emmy Award–Winning Actor

"A must-read for any teacher or prison administrator looking for criminal justice reform in the months ahead! Beth Rondeau's three years' experience in developing a functional and effective classroom atmosphere in a maximum-security prison is vividly outlined in this outstanding [book]. Ms. Rondeau shows us how she took over a loosely run educational program and turned it around to give each of her offender students the challenge of improving themselves through hard work and supportive learning from an exceptionally dedicated teacher. . . . You will not be the same educator or administrator once you have read this."

—HANS A. ANDREWS, EDD
Distinguished Fellow, President of Olney Central College (Ret.)

"I would like to commend Ms. Beth on her grit and tenacity in sticking to the already difficult calling of being a teacher in any situation. This book should be read by all educators, teachers, and administrators who really want to make an impact with their students and want to learn from a true professional."

—PROFESSOR CARLOS RONCAL
CEO and Founder, World Language Schools

"Beth takes you on a journey that is scary, heart-wrenching, and yet somehow brings an uplifting spirit. . . . She demonstrates that through pure passion for being an educator, much can be done to change our world and the world of those that are in prison. Kudos to Beth for bringing light and hope to make a better situation for those that we as society would rather forget. This is a must-read for an educator and all."

—WENDY RIVET-BRISLEY, EdD

"An astonishing masterpiece filled with compelling stories and life adventures of humanity . . . It is a book that can change your life and the people you love."

—LARRY LI
Mentor and Life Coach

"A remarkable story about how one woman changed—and saved—the lives of countless men who had lost hope."

—BONNIE HEARN HILL
Author

SEVEN DOORS IN

One Teacher's Mission within Prison Walls

BETH RONDEAU

BROWN BOOKS
PUBLISHING GROUP

Seven Doors In
One Teacher's Mission within Prison Walls

Brown Books Publishing Group
Dallas, TX / New York, NY
www.BrownBooks.com
(972) 381-0009

A New Era in Publishing®

Publisher's Cataloging-In-Publication Data

Names: Rondeau, Beth, author.
Title: Seven doors in : one teacher's mission within prison walls / Beth Rondeau.
Description: Dallas TX ; New York, NY : Brown Books Publishing Group, [2021]
Identifiers: ISBN 9781612545141
Subjects: LCSH: Rondeau, Beth. | Prison educators--Biography. | Prisoners--Education. | Teacher-student relationships. | LCGFT: Autobiographies.
Classification: LCC HV8875 .R66 2021 | DDC 365/.666--dc23

ISBN 978-1-61254-514-1
LCCN 2020923837

Printed in Canada
10 9 8 7 6 5 4 3 2 1

For more information or to contact the author, please go to www.7DoorsIn.com.

To all my former students.
As much as I have taught you, I have learned
from you. I am forever grateful for all the ways
you've helped me to grow as a teacher.

Contents

Note

This memoir is based on the author's recollection of real-life events. The names and identifying details of the offenders and prison employees in the account have been changed in order to protect their privacy, and the book should be regarded as a subjective account written from the perspective of a single individual. While some details may not be accurate, the author has striven to ensure that her experiences and perspective on the change she witnessed during her three years as a teacher in a maximum-security prison school are as true to life as possible with respect to human error.

Acknowledgments

I live my life in gratitude to the memory of my mother and father, Ann and Royal Rondeau. They instilled in me the values I follow to this day—a strong work ethic, a kind heart, a positive voice, the courage to follow my beliefs, and the understanding of the value of a good education.

I would also like to say thank you to the late Mr. Adolph Passint, my high school algebra teacher, who inspired me to enter the field of mathematics. I am also grateful to former minimum-security instructor Sue Dunlay for her ear and expertise in the lonely prison education world. Her friendship has meant a lot to me.

I would like to thank attorney Curtis Dial for his expertise and legal counsel, as well as Terence Gordon and TNG Films for believing, inquiring, and caring enough about my journey to want to share some of it with the world.

I owe additional thanks to many people who helped during the writing of this book and during the time period it is written about—to the correctional officers who supported me and taught me so much about the workings of the prison system; to my friend and colleague Ruth Ann Ritter, who was there for me when I was frustrated and needed extra support to keep writing; to my sister-in-law, Christine Rondeau, whose efforts helped coalesce my thoughts and stories into this book; and to my family, who were supportive and patient, especially my daughter Lucy, to whom I owe the title. I appreciate you all. Finally, a thanks to my publisher, Brown Books Publishing Group, for their help in bringing my story to the world.

Introduction

*"Our lives begin to end the day we become
silent about things that matter."*
—Martin Luther King Jr.

BE BRAVE ENOUGH TO MAKE A CHANGE

As I drive by the old prison, which sits empty now, I think about my
first trek down the sidewalk into "the Walls." At that old, imposing
prison, reminiscent of a castle fortress, I set out on a journey that would
forever change my life. Driving by again now, I think how fortunate I
was to take the job I took there. It gave me a new set of eyes and a new
appreciation for life.

Before I became a maximum-security prison teacher, I had never
known anyone serving time in prison. I had never been a victim of a
crime, nor had I known anyone who was. Still, as I walked through
Door Seven on my first day, it was with an open mind, no expectations,
and a clear understanding that these men were my students, people I
would not judge. I would not pity them or permit them to focus on
the misery of their pasts. In my classroom, I would give them only a
narrow one-way path to move forward, and, as in any classroom, we
would earn each other's respect.

However, after only a few days working with these men, these
offenders, I came to the realization that I was naive and sheltered. A
direct, no-frills midwesterner who grew up with parents who strongly

believed in helping others, I thought I knew about this world I was entering, but I was wrong. The men I now taught had grown up in environments that excluded them from experiencing true family lives with strong values. Many were so busy dodging bullets, selling drugs, stealing, and using survival techniques to live that they never experienced nine-to-five jobs, holiday celebrations, home-cooked meals, proper educations, or just building the reasoning skills the rest of us take for granted. Although experienced in teaching adult education classes in the free world, I had not been exposed to the vulgar language, the low cognitive abilities, and the people with truly rough upbringings I now encountered.

As a maximum-security prison teacher, I experienced some truly eye-opening moments. These moments could be as simple as lunch arriving late to class one day, when, instead of complaining that his meal wasn't hot, one of my students, Offender Flo, took the time to appreciate the food offered him in prison. "Back home," he told me, "I was lucky to get a piece of bread with mayonnaise on it."

I still remember the shocked look on Offender Cole's face when I told him I was forty-seven years old. His mouth dropped open, and his eyes widened. He asked me how I was still alive. He thought I must be joking about my age because he didn't have family members or friends who had survived that long.

The majority of my students in the Walls had lived lives just as difficult and stunted before going to prison. During my time with them, I heard many stories of survival on the streets. Their intense need for self-preservation continued after they were convicted and incarcerated. In the Walls, survival came first. Getting an education was much farther down on my students' lists, if it was on there at all.

Three years later, when I left the prison to teach in a public school system, these memories, among many others, traveled quietly along with me into my new classroom. They reminded me of the forgotten people in this world, people I used to consider out of sight, out of mind. They will never again be out of mind for me, and that is why I wrote this book: to bring them to your mind as well and hopefully show you the ways in which some people can change.

Often, during my time at the prison, I was asked, "How can you stand up there in front of murderers and rapists?"

Teachers from other schools asked the question. People in the community asked it. Most of all, family members and friends asked it. Here's what I replied:

"I don't stand in front of murders and rapists. I stand in front of my students."

I didn't know what their crimes were. I was there to teach. My students were in prison because of something they had done in the past. I was there to move them toward the future, to help them see their potential.

There is such hopelessness among those passing through the United States criminal justice system today. I want to add my voice to those calling to end it. Justice reform has become an increasingly important and popular topic in politics, and rightfully so. But it goes beyond emptying prisons that have become too full. I believe that our justice system should be reformed because people can change. Many who have grown up in their prison cells now deserve the grace of a second chance.

Once, I didn't understand, know, or care what happens in prison. You may be like I was then. I hope this book gives you a feel for why the voice for justice reform continues to grow. Come inside those steel doors with me; share in the experiences of the people I called my students. Perhaps then you will comprehend why, in some cases, we should forgive and move forward.

All of us understand that we ourselves have hurt others in the past. When we look back with shame and regret on our sins and on our mistakes, at times the only way for us to go on is to tell ourselves that we have changed, that we are not the people who did those things anymore.

In the same way that we forgive ourselves, we can forgive those our justice system sentenced to prison when time and maturity have turned them into different people.

In some cases, experiencing success in prison can give our offenders the chance of a better future: the ability to solve problems, the confidence to help others, the maturity to accept failures, the desire to improve, and the knowledge to truly enjoy being part of something bigger than themselves. But if our justice system does not give them that same chance to practice what they have learned outside of the prison walls, they have no hope of reintegrating into society and sharing what they have learned.

I am curious. Do you think people can change? Can you read this book with an open mind and let change into your own heart? I truly believe some of our currently incarcerated offenders deserve to walk in the free world again. Let me tell you what convinced me: the things I observed behind Door Seven during my three years as a maximum-security prison teacher.

1

The Long Walk to Door Seven

He who opens a school door, closes a prison.
—Victor Hugo

ENTRANCE DAY

Have you ever suddenly found that there's a sharp right turn in the road ahead, and you could swear that there was no warning sign? Well, my sharp right turn led me to that first day in the Walls. With it came a major change in my educational career.

The days of chaperoning dances, calling parents, listening to teenage drama, and attending pep assemblies ended when I accepted the challenge to teach men in a maximum-security prison. Instead of standing in front of teenagers seven hours a day, I would now stand facing murderers, rapists, kidnappers, drug dealers, and the mentally ill. I would walk into an environment where I was constantly watched, not only by security but by the inmates. I would discipline my students with consequential minor and major reports, resulting in, at the least, loss of privileges and, at the worst, solitary confinement in—in the prison vernacular—"the hole."

I would watch for gang paraphernalia, contraband, and shanks. When my students were confined to their cells, or their "homes," I would teach through the steel bars. I would be exposed to blood-filled fights and the strong fumes of pepper spray. I would also reach my new students as I had never before reached anyone.

At 6:45 a.m. on that first day, I entered the parking lot of the maximum-security prison that would house my classroom for the next year. The parking lot was spacious, but there were only a few spots available, far from the sidewalk entrance. I saw uniformed officers walking to and from their vehicles. As I stepped out of my car, many took notice. I was a newbie, and my civilian clothes stood out. I wore light gray slacks with a black-and-silver belt, a black fitted undershirt covered by a half-buttoned, long-sleeved yellow silk blouse, and shiny black shoes with a slight heel. My straight brunette hair with blond highlights rested on my upper back just below my shoulders. The one commonality between myself and the officers was that we all carried a see-through lunch pail and keys. My phone could not enter the Walls, and so I left it locked in my car.

A large sign by the entrance welcomed me with this message:

> Lock all doors and windows before leaving vehicles.
> Vehicles are not to be left unattended while running.
> Random searches will be conducted.

I was not in Kansas anymore.

I could hear people talking, but I couldn't tell where their voices were coming from. Looking around, I noticed a fenced-in yard. As I approached the fence, the voices grew louder. About twenty men in green T-shirts and jeans looked up from the area on the other side of the fence. All wore white tennis shoes. Some sat at picnic tables, and others walked laps near the fence border or jogged while wearing earbuds. Many stopped what they were doing and watched me walk toward the sidewalk, which led not only to the prison entrance but past the penned-in area where they congregated. Some waved and hollered, "Good morning," and I reciprocated. *They must be minimum-security inmates*, I thought.

Two men continued walking on the opposite side of the fence in the same direction as I did. I looked up at them. "Good morning, guys," I said. "It's going to be a hot one today. Supposed to be in the high nineties."

They smiled. "Yes, ma'am," one of them said. "Are you a new counselor?"

"No," I replied, "I am the new teacher."

"Well," one of them said. "I hope your first day is a good one."

"I'm looking forward to it," I told him. "You guys have a good day."

I continued to the front of the prison and glanced one more time at the fenced-in offenders, noticing the two men I just spoke with were then walking over to the picnic tables where all the others were congregating.

As I continued what seemed like a lengthy walk, I noticed more men wearing green shirts and blue jeans loading into a white Correctional Department van. I later learned these minimum-security offenders worked at "outs" jobs and were heading to the local parks to cut the grass and clean. The sidewalk continued past the entrance door. I stopped and gazed up at the outside of the high stone prison walls with concertina wire around the top. I'd have a hard time imagining a more foreboding entrance.

A group of officers, all dressed in brown uniforms with shiny black boots, exited the main entrance. They looked tired, yet they were very friendly. Some wore brown baseball hats, and others were bareheaded. One looked at me and said, "Be safe, Teach."

"Thank you, sir," I replied, wondering how he knew I was the new teacher.

A couple of breakfast trays sat on top of a garbage can near the entrance. Two men wearing bright green shirts and jeans exited the building. When they noticed me, they smiled and nodded. Both were wearing plastic gloves. They picked up the trays and emptied the garbage can. They were minimum-security grounds workers, and they were responsible for mowing the exterior lawn and the warden's lawn across the street from the prison. They also cleaned the offices in the main building where employees entered each day.

Everyone seemed friendly and respectful, and so my first impression was a positive one. Still, I reminded myself that the people I had encountered thus far were either going home for the day or were minimum-security offenders, men who would one day be free again. I wondered what the atmosphere would be like once I was inside the Walls. Would the offenders be this friendly? Would the guards be stern and mean? How would they feel about the offenders getting a free education? Would they support my efforts to help these men? Listening to community members, I had learned many did not feel men in prison deserved an education. Why should taxpayers pay me to educate criminals? Since the majority of my students were sentenced to die in prison, why bother educating them?

I didn't care about any of these concerns. This was my job. My new students were serving sentences for their transgressions, but I was not there to judge them. I didn't feel any ill will toward them. Our only connection would be the one between teacher and students.

I walked in the front entrance door and saw a female officer standing, watching the scanner as employees lined up, removed their coats, shoes, and belts, and placed them, along with their see-through lunch pails, on the moving belt. Then, they walked through a metal detector. The officers were talkative, and I noticed quickly that they addressed each other by last names. They wore their badges pinned to the left front pocket of their uniforms, and their steel-toed black boots were shiny.

One of them looked at me from a short distance and nodded. I heard him ask the other officers who I was.

"The new teacher," another one replied. "Her picture was just emailed to us all yesterday morning."

Another asked the door officer if there had been any activity yesterday evening.

She responded, "Only one small fight. A rather quiet night."

I had been instructed earlier by the treatment director to go directly to the human resource office to pick up my badge. On my way there, I walked past the sterile-looking personal-effects lockers of the employees and visitors. An open area contained a couple of well-worn couches outside the office, where I was instructed to sit and wait for the other fully trained teacher. They wouldn't allow me to enter the Walls alone until I completed a four-week orientation, which would include life-saving and self-defense training.

Nearby, a ruckus brought the conveyer belt line to come to a halt. Watching, I saw that a lunchbox was being searched because the scanner showed contraband inside.

"There's nothing in my lunchbox. That's just the scanner giving its usual false-positive results," the officer joked as his lunchbox was searched. "Good to keep you on your toes though."

Some of the other officers looked at the screen to see what the scanner showed. And still others, more experienced, just waited their turn in line, a little irritated by the hold up. Quickly, I got a feel for the new versus the experienced officers. The screen was programmed to randomly show prohibited items to make sure the operators were attentive. This time, it showed a sleeping mask, the kind you put over your eyes to keep out the light. That is considered contraband, but it was not found in the lunchbox. The programmed-in false positive had accomplished its intended purpose.

The other teacher, Erin, arrived. I was excited to finally enter the prison. We placed our items on the belt to be scanned and took our turn to walk through the metal detector. We quickly put our shoes and belts back on, and we then followed the line of trained officers up the stairs to the second floor, where we waited for our turn to enter a code to retrieve our keys for that day.

I could see the first entrance ahead of me. I didn't quite know how I was feeling at this point, but I noticed many stares, and I was sure the officers were wondering how long I would stay at the prison. Most teachers didn't last long. The pay is low, and the danger is high.

As the only two in the group dressed in civilian clothes, Erin and I kept receiving advice from the officers as we slowly approached the first door.

"Just be yourself."

"Treat the men with respect, and they will be respectful."

"But remember where you are, and just be smart."

My mouth went a little dry. "Thank you, sir," I replied automatically.

The seven steel doors I was about to pass through would correlate, over the next few years, to the process I would undergo with my new students—a series of breakthroughs and "Aha!" moments as the doors of their minds opened to learning, teamwork, constructive competition, true self-respect, and more.

THE FIRST DOOR

The short walk down the hall included a half-wall that allowed for one last glimpse of the outside front entrance—the last sight of the free world. Everything beyond was prison.

Erin and I stood by the first locked door, which was imposingly large and made of yellow metal. We waited for an officer to allow us entrance. The security was high and intense. Only eight people at a time were welcomed through the first door. It slid open with a thud, and we approached a window.

Next, we showed our badges to an officer who was enclosed behind bulletproof glass. He put a radio in a drawer under his window and slid it out to us. We were assigned that specific black radio, which was tagged with our last names. When we spoke over the radio, officers, shift captains, the warden, security, doctors, nurses, counselors, and anyone else working in the prison—offenders included—could hear what we said. The radio had a red button to alert everyone of an emergency. As soon as the button was pushed, the control center would know who needed help.

No one was allowed to enter the prison without a radio, because our lives could depend on its use. Our ability to communicate and call for help if we needed it was our life support. The radio I received at the first door was a stark reminder that the students I was excited to meet would be unlike any students I had met before.

We were given specific instructions on how to call for help, when to push the emergency button, and what specifically to say. In an emergency, there is little time to speak because the radios need to be open for responses and other security communications. "Tell us who you are, where you are, and give us a quick rundown of what's happening," they told us. If we were ever in a situation where we couldn't speak, we had to hit the emergency button to alert the command center to our location.

The Second Door

We had to wait for all eight people to receive radios before the second yellow metal door heavily slid open. As the final member of our group entered the hallway, the sound of the door sliding into its lock echoed behind us. "Hey, Teach," one of the officers called. His tone was serious. "Keep that radio on at all times. If you sense any danger, hit the button, and we'll be there. Don't worry about hitting it too often. Remember where you are! It is better to be safe than sorry. Follow your gut feeling, always."

He went on, "You will be all right, but just be aware of your surroundings. There are cameras in the classroom. And the doorman and shift captains will be watching you. We will take care of you. You will be on camera always unless you are using the bathroom. Be smart, and stay alert at all times. I can't say that enough."

I heard myself give another automatic reply. "Got it. Thank you, sir." This was definitely turning out to be more than just another day at school, I thought.

I looked up for the cameras the officer had mentioned. Sure enough, there they were, positioned at intervals all along the hallway.

THE THIRD DOOR

At the end of the tiny hallway, I could see a third imposing yellow metal door, only wide enough for two people to walk side by side. As Erin and I approached the end of the hallway, this third door opened with the same resounding thud. We walked through the opening, and I heard yet another layer of security fall in place behind us, increasing the divide between us and the free world. Again, I looked up and saw cameras on the left and right corners of the ceilings. And somehow, this brought me a sense of security in this strange, new world.

As each door closed, the conversations diminished. People were only speaking a few words now this far into the prison. Our group made a right turn and walked toward the street side of the original construction prison walls.

THE FOURTH DOOR

We came to the fourth door, which was surprisingly left open. Offenders were entering to receive their morning medications at the infirmary window. They were quite respectful as they said good morning to us. I got many stares because I was a newcomer to their home.

"Who are you?" someone asked.

I replied, "The new teacher."

We then walked through the fourth door outside to the yard. I looked up at the tall buildings, which included the cell houses, administration office building, chow hall, prison industries building, and another building that housed an indoor gym and library. The shift captain's office, surrounded by many windows, was to the right.

I walked out onto the sidewalk. As I looked up, I saw towers where sharpshooters were positioned. Again, I noticed cameras up on the outside corners of the buildings. At this point, we were totally enclosed, and I could not see out to the street. Crooked, broken sidewalks led to the various buildings. In the far end of the yard, I saw the outdoor weight room, the basketball court, the track, and the softball field. Some things were in working order. Others were in desperate need of repair. The strange dichotomy continued all the way across the yard—a beautifully groomed lawn contrasting with a row of fenced-in cages, about three men wide, where "lockup" men spent their solitary single hour of yard time, situated within the prison yard with the razor wire surrounding all of them.

It was a short distance to the administration building where the school was located. As Erin and I walked, I was surprised to observe an immaculate flower garden by the stairway. I saw one of the offenders working in it, watched by the armed guards stationed in the towers. The offender welcomed us with a smile and a pleasant good morning. I complimented his vibrant garden.

The Fifth Door

We continued our walk up to the doors to the administration building, which houses the treatment director, security warden, deputy warden, and some administrative assistants. As we had been instructed, we continually paused to check behind us. We then proceeded to unlock the fifth door with a key, enter the building, check once more behind us, then secure the door again.

In this building, I came to learn, the treatment director oversaw religious groups, the school, the antiviolence program, the Thinking for a Change Program, and the arts and crafts program, along with any other programs brought to the prison. If a specific group needed special food because of a religious fast or for other reasons, he informed all employees what to do. He was also the supervisor for the counselors. He worked with the security warden when deciding and scheduling tours.

The security warden was in charge of the security for the entire prison. She decided what new security measures would be enforced. When I brought in a world map, the security warden looked over the map closely to make sure there were no highways or other roads noted on it before she approved it. The security warden also had to approve magazines before I was able to bring them in for school. She needed to be sure there was no nudity or any articles that would show men how to make weapons.

She also had the final say of when and how long the prison would be locked down. If it was foggy outside and the sharpshooters couldn't see a certain distance, the offenders were placed on restrictive movement, which meant they could leave their cells only if shackled and with an escort. Any movement must be authorized as absolutely necessary— to see a doctor, for example. If not, it was denied during restrictive movement.

The deputy warden was second in command of the prison. The secretaries housed in the building worked for these three wardens and took care of employee payroll. The warden's office was located outside of the Walls at the entrance building. His incoming presence was announced over the radio every time he entered the Walls, and the sharpshooters stood outside their towers whenever the warden was inside the Walls or if groups were touring the premises.

THE SIXTH DOOR

As I looked down the hall, I could see the sixth door. This one also needed to be opened with a key. We opened that door, locking it behind us, of course.

We turned to our left, and there it was: the seventh door.

THE SEVENTH DOOR

Behind the seventh door was the school. It was so very different from the classrooms in which I had taught for the past twenty years.

I immediately noticed more cameras in the corners of the school. It was stark and bare, consisting of only two rooms. The smaller one to the right included two metal cages, each barely big enough to contain a single desk and a chair. In the main area, there were two 1960s-era metal teacher's desks, an old wooden teacher's desk, a couple of filing cabinets, five tables with chairs around them, some bookshelves, and five computer hubs. The stark white walls contained little other than a few words of encouragement:

"To succeed, you need a work ethic."

"Help others grow."

There weren't any whiteboards or blackboards in the classroom. How would I teach my classes? Where would we congregate to discuss problems?

With the peeling paint, this didn't look like a place with an atmosphere for learning. I saw only a few books on the shelf. The two shelves in the room were cluttered with packets of papers. One wall was all windows. Through the windows, I could see what appeared to be a hut, and around that area, there was a rope that set the boundary around it.

"What is that?" I asked Erin.

She explained that it was a sweat lodge the Native American inmates used for their weekly ritual. The rope boundary marked off where no one was to walk on their sacred grounds. She mentioned how the elderly teacher I replaced hadn't liked its location. One day, it was so windy that the tarp over the hut blew off, and she could see all the naked men sitting in there. She was quite embarrassed, which greatly entertained her students.

There were two doors in the school, and they were both kept locked. The men entered through the opposite classroom door. I realized I would be locked in the classroom with my students. It didn't seem to make sense, but then I realized that there were only about eight to twelve men in school each hour of the day. There were over 750 on the other side of the door. Once I walked in the seventh door, I was locking myself in with murderers, rapists, and other felons. The men housed in this maximum-security prison were supposedly the worst of the worst. Erin would only be teaching with me approximately four more months before I completely took over the school duties on my own. Yet, I still was not scared.

Erin took me downstairs because I wanted to get a glimpse of the chapel and the offices. Much to my disappointment, the chapel was just an empty room with chairs. All the offices and rooms were so plain; very bare with not much to look at. There were only the essentials like paper, pencils, computers, and other office supplies. Nothing to make the offices feel warm.

It was now approximately 7:20 a.m., and my first students arrived at 7:30. These students came from Unit One, which housed new offenders and those who were making their way back up the tier from lockup. A couple of students were also due to arrive from lockup. These men were only allowed to move with shackles and double escorts. Those in lockup were only allowed schooling if they were under twenty-one years of age. I will repeat this: only if they were under age twenty-one! And their restraints did not come off until they were in one of those two metal cages.

It is important for you to know that while I taught in this maximum-security prison, there was never a fight in the school. It would become known as the "safe zone." There had been a fight in the school just three weeks before I arrived. The two men involved were in lockup. Erin had forgotten to turn on her radio that day, and Tim, the chapel officer, finally heard the scuffle when tables and desks started crashing. Erin thought she was hitting the button to call for help, but no help arrived. Officer Tim came running from downstairs and shouted, "Why aren't you hitting your button?" Erin told him she did hit her button, but the alarm didn't go off. Tim hit his own button, and soon the Critical Emergency Response Team arrived. CERT is a special team of officers, two of them with K9 dogs who are trained specifically for emergencies.

After things settled and the men were shackled and removed, Erin realized her radio hadn't been on. She had had a meeting earlier that day in the educational office, which was located outside the Walls, so she had shut her radio off and forgot to turn it back on. No one noticed the fight until the alarm went off. Erin's account of the event made me realize that even with so many cameras in the prison, not every camera was watched continuously.

As I looked out the window, I saw men walking along the sidewalk. I wondered whether they were coming to school, going to work, or heading to the chapel. The majority of the men did work in the prison; some in prison industries making furniture, others the chow hall, library, school, laundry, grounds, or cleaning throughout the prison. Soon I would see which would be my students. There were two young men in shackles and orange jumpsuits. The others were in white T-shirts and jeans. They had smiles on their faces as they talked to each other. As I watched them, I was again surprised to realize I felt no fear, only the usual excitement to meet my students on the first day at a new school.

Behind the closed and locked seventh door in the Walls, my teaching career was opened to a new frontier. Behind that closed and locked seventh door, I found the greatest opportunity I had yet seen to make a difference.

2

Passing the Test

Though no one can go back and make a brand-new start,
anyone can start from now and make a brand-new ending.
—**Carl Bard**

That first day of classes, I anxiously watched through the school windows as the men walked single-file down the uneven sidewalk. There were about twelve in the first group, followed by the two young lockup students accompanied by guards. These last two were following farther behind, their steps hampered by their heavy leg chains.

I noticed a look of excitement on the men's faces as they drew near. Those coming to school already knew they would meet their new teacher today. One thing is for sure: in prison, news travels quickly! From the moment I walked toward the front door of the prison and told the men in minimum security that I was the new teacher, the news immediately spread through both prisons. Even those in "the hole" knew I was there.

As they were getting closer, I found myself wondering about their sentences. Which men were sentenced to life without parole, a sentence that was basically that of death in confinement? Which students would have the opportunity to see the free world again? Perhaps it may seem strange, but this first day, I did not wonder about the nature of these men's crimes. What brought each of them to this place was in the past, as far as I was concerned. Each of the men would open up and share his story with me over the next few months as I gained his trust. But I came to the school in the Walls as a teacher. My main concern was whether I would have the ability to help them succeed.

I used my key to unlock the seventh door so the men could enter the classroom. As my students walked in, we greeted each other with smiles and quiet good mornings. Each student quickly took his seat. Some immediately went to the computer hubs, put on headphones, and began listening to music. Others sat around tables talking, occasionally looking down at the work in front of them. The one commonality was that they all took turns watching me, some with curiosity and others with veiled distrust. They were sizing me up, learning what they could about me from the way I dressed, how I acted, and how I carried myself. The ability to quickly size up and assess someone new is a vital skill in prison—and one I would also learn.

Soon, the corrections officers, or COs, as they are commonly known, brought in the two students dressed in orange jumpsuits. They also greeted me with smiles as I welcomed them to school. I followed behind as the COs took them to the partitioned room, locking them in the cages anchored to the floor. Each contained a writing desk and had room enough for one inmate only. These students' leg restraints were not taken off, but once each cage door was locked, the men stuck their hands out of a slit in the cages, and the officers removed the handcuffs. These students were then given papers and pencils.

I made sure to thank the officers for bringing these men to my classroom. I knew that the COs were not only bringing the students to school for me to teach but were also risking their lives by bring-ing them. These officers were there to protect me too. I respectfully addressed them as "sir" or "ma'am," always thanked them, and made sure to wish them a good day as a way to show my appreciation for all they were doing.

Next, as in most classrooms, it was time to take attendance. I needed to make sure there weren't any mistakes, because it was also my job to complete payroll for the students who attended. The men earned thirty cents for each hour of study, so I recorded the number of hours each day that they attended school. This may not seem like much, but the economics of a prison, like the inmates, are far removed from the outside world. The offenders are given clothes, jackets, shoes, blankets, toiletries, and a bed. But their hourly wages were used to buy very valuable extras: to rent or buy a television, snacks, an e-reader, phone calls, art supplies, magazines, and books.

On this first day, as I walked around the room, the men extended their hands to greet me. As I told them my name, I thanked them for coming to class.

There was so much I wanted to say to my new students, but I kept it simple and said how great it was that they wanted to improve their education. As I spoke to them, they discussed me among themselves. They didn't even try to whisper.

Finally, one of them came out and asked me a direct question. "Where are you from?" They had quickly assessed that I wasn't a local. They attributed my accent to Canada.

"Close," I told them. I shared how I grew up in Michigan.

But I soon found that accents were not the only barrier to our communication. Another student spoke up. "My homies wanna know whatchya doin' here," he said. "You don't look like no prison worker. You got too much swag to be here."

I was unfamiliar with prison slang, and I struggled to understand this, but I simply looked the man right in the eyes and smiled. "We're going to get along just fine," I said, "and you all are going to get an education."

"What you smiling for?" he demanded in reply. "Nobody here is happy. Why you seem so happy?"

"I love teaching," I answered.

Another student asked, "You work with criminals before?"

As a matter of fact, I had, though never before anyone currently serving time for a crime. Before coming to the prison, I had taught adults back in Michigan. Many of them had previously been in jail, had drug abuse issues, or were considered low-income and wanted to turn their lives around. They had inspired me. They had come to school to better themselves, not because they were required to be there as high school students are.

So, I answered their queries, "You aren't criminals in my eyes. You are my students, and, as of today, that is how I will look at you every time you walk through that door." I pointed to the seventh door. "You are doing your time, and your crime is old news. Today begins your new lives."

My new students were wary. "Whatchya mean?"

"You are here, aren't you?" I asked.

The offenders just looked at me.

"That tells me you are ready for change. You are getting educated."

They looked at me and laughed. "We don't do nothin' in school," one said. "We listen to our music and do these damn worksheets all the time."

I thought about this. "Not anymore," I said with a smile.

The men looked at each other, trying to figure me out. *Who is this woman? What is she up to?* I noticed some of them nodding at their classmates.

That first day, when the men left, some said, "Make sure you got my hours. Don't mess up my pay. That's all I got." The words weren't threatening, and others around them smiled as they said them. And as the students grew more confident over the months I taught them, they began to talk less about money and more about passing tests.

My students were as diverse as they come—black, white, Hispanic, and Native American. However, as they themselves pointed out to me, the population was disproportionate to demographics outside. They insisted the justice system is truly corrupt. The majority inside the prison was black or Latino. I paid attention, and as time went on, I noticed that they were right. Most of my students were Hispanic or black. I began to wonder why that was.

I paid close attention to everything my students said, not only out of curiosity but also for security reasons. I was reminded of what I had been told earlier in the day: "Be safe, and stay alert." Some of my students wanted to speak to each other in Spanish. I put a stop to that immediately. If I couldn't understand what they were saying, none of us would be safe. School was not going to be a place for the men to discuss their gang activity. One student didn't speak any English, so he was an exception. One of my tutors spoke Spanish, and he was assigned to help that student. I did not allow the other students to speak with him in class. I had to have some trust, yet I knew to balance that by showing that I was aware.

A few students spoke very little English, which was also a challenge. I didn't want to disrespect them, and I tried hard to understand their words. Sometimes the slang was more difficult than the Spanish. Some of the common prison terms and phrases I heard that first day included the following: "we down for some time," "my home boys," "homies," "banging in the yard," "dope," "I feel ya," "skinheads," "shanks," "Crips," "gay for the stay," "mafia," "turf," "piece," "snitch," "rat," "kite," and "bible."

The men had many different nicknames for each other: Locks, Shootery, Redneck, Slim, Cat, and so on. Later I learned that by using nicknames, they would not be able to admit anything when asked specifically about an inmate identified by his surname. If they didn't know the real names of the other inmates, they would be unable to confess anything about them. That was the reason they gave me for using nicknames so preferentially, at least. At times, I got the feeling they didn't want to remember their real names.

Erin, the teacher I had followed into the prison school that morning, worked with the men in the cages. Both of the students from the hole that first day were young black men between the ages of eighteen and twenty who had educational plans that required extra attention in both math and reading. A part-time special education teacher had also worked with them, but he was available for only a couple of hours a day, so, in the future, I would still work with them as a regular education teacher.

I sat with Erin in chairs outside the confinement cages to discuss the students' work with them. They soon let me know that if they served their time in confinement without any issues, they could work their way up the prison's tier system and come to class like everyone else.

I asked each why they were in solitary confinement. They both were confined there due to a fight in the chow hall. "Miss Teacher Lady, we will be out soon, and then we can come to class with Unit One," said the one in the left cage. "We both done almost thirty days in the hole. Please give us as much time in school as possible. We only get out for school and an hour in the pen [a three-person-wide exercise cage]."

"You work hard," I told him, "and I will see about giving you more time in school."

Troy came in to begin working with them, so I told them we would work together later.

I went back to the other part of the classroom and walked around the room, offering assistance. I could hear the men candidly talking about me again, and they weren't shy about it. One man said I was "thick," and another said I looked like I was about thirty years old. That got a smile out of the forty-something me. Another man commented on my jewelry and quickly learned from my charm bracelet that I was married and had three kids. I decided not to wear that bracelet again.

They continued making observations, some of them unnerving. They commented on the nice shoes I wore, jokingly referring to my red Naturalizers as "boatman's shoes." Another said I dressed too fancy, and that I didn't fit in. It sounded like my clothing led them to think that perhaps I was an FBI agent working undercover.

The offenders had a strange, indirect way of speaking. They knew that complimenting a prison employee directly was grounds for a minor report action against them, so they talked about me right in front of me without speaking directly to me. I continued to walk around, getting the men on task and working. I ignored their comments, presenting as though they didn't affect me. I later learned that the men called me Agent B while in the yard, because some truly believed I was working for the FBI. This misconception just meant I had a longer road to walk to win their trust.

Once I had everyone on task and working, I sat at my desk, looking through my materials and listening to the men talk. They seemed not to realize I was listening. Not that it would have mattered to them. But I also genuinely wasn't upset by their talking. I was new, after all, and just what else would they have to talk about? I could tell that their conversation wasn't as much disrespectful as it was curious. I still decided not to share most of it with my family at the dinner table.

All the men returned to their cells for a count, and that is when I ate lunch. After the count, I could see more men heading in the direction of the school. A couple of students I hadn't seen yet arrived at Door 7. My reputation had already preceded me.

As soon as they walked in, one said, "Miss Beth, why aren't you scared of us? Who are you?"

I just laughed. I was quickly learning that my attitude was a rarity here. I came in with a positive attitude, a teacher's attitude. "I haven't done anything to you, so why should I be scared?" I asked them. "I am just here to help." I shook their hands and said, "Come on in. We are going to learn something today."

I remember quite clearly the first man I worked with that day. He raised his hand and asked for help with his math work. I volunteered before Erin had a chance. I didn't like just sitting around; I wanted to teach. I had been in the classroom for only an hour, and I already realized the days could be long.

This young black man, Flynn, was sitting at one of the computer hubs. As I walked over, he slid one of the earphones away from his ear. I grabbed a chair and sat down next to him. I looked down at the problem and the work he had done to complete it. I asked for his pencil so I could show him his error. Then I asked him to complete another problem so I could watch to make sure he truly understood the process, just as I had done with all of my other students throughout my career. He hesitated but then took back his pencil, started in on the new problem, and solved it. When I complimented him, he slipped both earphones down around his neck and redoubled his efforts. He asked me about a few other problems he had struggled with in the past, and we went over them together. As a teacher, I didn't think too much of this. But for Flynn, this exchange meant a whole lot more.

When we were done, he looked at me and said, "You aren't scared. You aren't even nervous. Why?"

For me, it was simple. "I am here to teach, not to judge," I told him. "And I mean no disrespect. I don't care what brought you here. I only care where you go from this point on."

His guarded expression changed into a smile, and I knew at that instant that I had passed his test. That was as big a moment to me as that math problem he had solved just moments ago was to him!

My answer to his question had surprised him, and I knew my other students were listening. I had surprised them all. They were struggling to understand why I was being so nonjudgmental. They were not used to this kind of treatment—many felt that everyone was against them, whether or not this was true.

Once I showed Flynn that I believed in him, he suddenly had faith that he could indeed graduate. He honestly admitted that math was a struggle. He knew it was difficult to find math teachers to work in prisons, but his success with a problem that had tripped him up unlocked a door in him. He opened up a little to me and talked with me a little about his family and life.

Flynn didn't have much time left in school. He would pass his math test in October and then complete his final test quickly afterward. He was scheduled to attend a graduation ceremony in December at the prison, the first I would attend.

That December, I stood up and announced the graduates at the ceremony. I didn't know many of the students well yet. I said a few words, mainly about Flynn. I shared with those in attendance how he had been the first student I had worked with in the Walls, and how his respect for me and our progress together confirmed for me that I was indeed where I needed to be. He became the prime example that justified the work I was doing.

I had the privilege to meet Flynn's mother that graduation day. What an amazing, supportive woman! She thanked me for helping her son, and I told her that although I was new, from what I had heard and observed about her son, he was helping himself by strengthening his determination and work ethic. She smiled. I told her to be proud because she had a respectful young man who had made a start on turning his life around and will continue to do so. She said he was a good kid but just made a bad decision one night. He had been doing well in school and wanted to go to college.

I said, "Well, now he has that opportunity, especially with your support." I walked Flynn's mother to the door, and she left a proud mom. Flynn was in prison for robbery, and after two years down (two years in prison), he would be able to leave in another year. His mom, a nurse, was his inspiration. He wanted to earn an engineering degree and play some basketball in college.

It was an inspiration to me to be the teacher that allowed Flynn to make that final mile and reach his graduation—and more, to pass his test—but he was far from the only student to inspire me.

That first graduation day, most of my students stayed for the majority of the day, sharing stories about their lives and struggles with school.

One student, Robs, told me my first day of teaching that he would be homebound in a few months but could never graduate. He didn't believe he could pass the math test, and when he was released, "home" for him would be a shelter. He had no family, and without an education or relatives to support him, what chance did he have to succeed?

Flynn had a future, but Robs gave me a definitive goal. His story reached me that first day, and I committed myself to working extra hard to show him that he was worth something. He was in desperate need of a diploma. An education could change his life. By the time October came, he knew he needed to finish his GED by January, not only because he would be paroled in January but also because the GED testing was ending. The prison's educational program was switching over to the HSED, and anyone who had not completed their GED would need to start over with all the tests. Robs knew that earning his GED was his only hope for success because he had no support on the outside. A GED could give him a vital chance to convince someone to take a chance on him and give him a job. We vowed to work together to get him through his last two tests, because Robs already knew what the others had yet to learn: education is the key to change. Amazing things were about to happen in the Walls's prison school, and it would be my privilege to lead the way.

3

Bruised Ribs

Failure will never overtake me if my
determination to succeed is strong enough.
—Og Mandino

I was determined to succeed in my new position, but for the first few weeks, I lived in ignorance of just what it was I had gotten into. Before my first day, I received a tour of the prison. The guards told me how dangerous the work could potentially be, but I had a nothing-will-happen-to-me attitude. I was a teacher who only wanted to help. Why would anyone want to hurt me?

Then one day, I was teaching a writing class when I heard a loud alarm coming from my radio, and I saw officers running down the hall. The chatter started coming in over the radio. "Two offenders fighting, Industries lunchroom"; "There is an ambulance on the way."

They kept a stretcher on the carpet wing near my classroom. Soon, an officer ran in and grabbed it. He went running back down the hall with it, and the radio kept blaring: "We are clearing out the Industries building"; "All industry workers are to be sent back to their pods."

Officer Dan came down to the school. "Men, I want you to head up to the arts and crafts room. We are going to restricted movement." The men gathered their possessions and started heading out.

After all the men were locked down, I went up front, and the officers were watching the fight in replay on the cameras. There was blood everywhere. I saw one offender knocked unconscious, and the second offender ignoring orders and continuing to attack him as the officers pulled him away. The unconscious man died from his injuries a couple weeks later. It was the first time I had seen a fight like that, and it made it clear to me just how vital it was that I be prepared for danger.

There was a mandatory safety and self-defense training course for everyone who worked in the prison, but when I began teaching, there was a class already in progress, so I had to wait for the next one to begin. For my safety, the first two weeks I worked at the prison, Erin remained in the classroom. I was not permitted to go anywhere inside the prison without her or an officer present.

The first morning of training, I was nervous. The corrections officers had warned me that the training would be very intense. There were weekly tests that I would be required to pass in order to progress and a graduation ceremony at the end. By the end of the five-week course, I would theoretically be prepared for anything I might encounter in the prison, walking over the units, walking around the yard, in the infirmary, chow hall, or lockup—pretty much anywhere the offenders were.

I would have to be prepared for any number of hypothetical worst-case scenarios. I had to consider what I might do if my officer was out doing rounds and something went down in the classroom. I had to consider what I might do if my officer got taken down in a fight, if all the officers in the unit got taken down. I had to be ready and able to defend myself for at least a couple of minutes until someone could get to me. That may not seem long, but when you're in crisis, minutes can seem like an eternity.

Offenders are very strong, and they also enjoy lifting weights. Most of them are in extremely good physical condition and could do a hundred horizontal pushups on a bar like nobody's business, so I had to learn to defend myself against that kind of strength. And I had to be aware that my students were the kind of men capable of taking the lives of others using nothing more than their own hands and brute strength.

I did not have to go into work each day expecting this to happen, or to happen to me. But I had to be aware of the danger.

My training included courses in self-defense, situational awareness, personal restraints, pat-downs, cell searches, gang identification and signals, drug awareness, and K9-unit awareness, just to name a few. Many prison employees begin the self-defense course, drop out, and seek other work as they come to realize the profound uncertainty and unpredictability of their work environment. The self-defense training is intense and involves full-on physical contact, which included trained K9 dogs demonstrating their abilities. Until a trained K9 dog is hanging off your arm, you won't believe the amount of strength police dogs possess. I was really thankful for the training pads.

My fellow students in the course included officers from several other prisons in the state. We were all expected to dress in business attire or uniform, depending on our jobs, except on days we trained in self-defense. Looking across the room my first day, I saw only three other civilians two other teachers and a nurse. I had entered into an entirely different world.

WEEK ONE

The entire first week of training was devoted to understanding what it meant to work in a prison. We were educated on the reality of prison riots and prison riot survival, and I was told that if there was ever a riot at my place of employment, my life would not be exchanged for the release of an offender.

We watched videos of a riot in another prison and saw with our own eyes how employees had been forced to place bags over their heads and stand in front of the windows wearing the offenders' T-shirts and jeans so that if snipers took a shot, they would shoot an employee, not an offender. We listened to a true story of one woman who was held captive for three days in a tower taken over by two offenders. She was forced to have sex with them over and over again. The only thing that worked was when she finally quit fighting them and they lost interest in her. We watched many more brutally honest videos of what could happen in a maximum-security environment. For some, it was all too real. There were law enforcement officers that quit after the first day of training when faced with the brutal, harsh reality of some of the worst-case scenarios.

There was one prison employee who had a panic attack after viewing the training videos. She later told me how, afterward, she went out to her car and cried. After a few days of the prison's mandatory training, she realized prison work was not for her. She visited the prison school one day and was too scared to continue working. I understood and agreed with her decision to leave. Working in a prison environment would have been detrimental to her mental health. It takes a certain kind of mental preparedness to work in a prison.

In another training session that first week, we were told to fight as hard as we could to save ourselves from being killed—sometimes, they said, this might mean deciding to comply with a rapist if we found ourselves in a situation where we could not escape. For some rapists, we learned, the fight is the attraction. Fighting could make them angrier and actually increase our danger. It was better, they said, to avoid situations where we might be unable to escape a rapist. They taught us to be aware of our surroundings at all times. They advised us that the only places there were not cameras were in the restrooms and told us to never open a door without looking behind us. They trained us never to show weakness or lack of confidence. Not only could it lead men to attack us, they might target us for less physically dangerous but definitely unpleasant con games.

We toured some other prisons near the training site and learned about the various programs each prison had in place. I noticed that those with less security offered more programs. For example, the medium-security prisons allowed inmates to train dogs for the blind. It was good for the men to learn to take care of the dogs because many had never taken care of anything in their lives. They learned to love their furry students, but then they also learned how painful it was to say goodbye when the training was complete.

There was even more freedom of movement in the lower-security prisons. The offenders in these facilities could work outside jobs. However, there were still count times throughout the day where the working men would need to report back to their cells, where steel doors once again closed behind them. The officers would then go around and count all the inmates. The officers would actually scan the inmates' badges from inside their cells as they were standing for the count. For counts during the night, officers always needed to see the inmates' faces. Sometimes, resting or sleeping offenders would have to get up in order to be properly identified.

In lower-security prisons or lower-security areas of a prison, offenders could roam freely. Their cells might be locked only for count and might not even be locked through the night, but in maximum-security facilities, the offenders would have to have a pass to go anywhere but the chow hall, yard, gym, library, or barber.

Each unit had different yard-time allowances. This allotted time would not just include time spent in the actual prison yard but also included time spent going to the library, engaging in arts and crafts, working out at the gym, pod time, or visiting the barbershop. There was extra nonconfinement time allowed for work, chapel visits, religious services, the sweat lodge, or prison school—up to five hours, depending on the unit's regulations.

All the prisons offered vocational classes; however, minimum-security prisons offered more. For example, in minimum, offenders could become certified welders. In maximum, they might become certified cleaners or bakers. Among all the harsh realities I was confronted with throughout the duration of my training course, learning offenders were offered these vocational opportunities provided me with some much-needed good news. But the instructors warned us not everything we learned would be so easy.

The very next day, we began learning about gangs. It was important for us to know not only the names of the various gangs but also the various gang signs. If we were taken captive, we were told to pay close attention to the tattoos and language the offenders used. These details would help to describe the offenders if we were able to get out or get to a radio.

When there were shakedowns (thorough searches to uncover hidden drugs, for example), they explained they always searched for gang paraphernalia in the cells. The men's bibles (gang rules) or sketching would help the security staff if they were found. Gang fights, prison stabbings, or information leaks could lead to more shakedowns in prisons. That first week, we accompanied officers as they conducted random shakedowns at a prison.

We learned not to call prison cells "houses." Inmates were offended if their cell was called their house. Language like this puts an offender in with the lifers. Those who go to their "cells" feel they can be released into civilian life again. When "cells" become "houses" or "homes," offenders feel institutionalized.

We learned the warnings to watch for that indicated a prison might need to tighten security. An informant might let officers know that there was a hit out on a staff member or on another offender. (This happened a few times during my tenure in the Walls.) If the informant mentioned that a female officer or employee was going to get raped or that a Hispanic officer was a target, the prison would perform shakedowns more often. Of course, the officers needed to protect not only the employees but the prison inmates too. Although the offenders were there serving time for their transgressions, they were not to be punished, officially or unofficially, for anything more if they were in the clear. Some officers had difficulties with this. We are all human, and those that became familiar with the crimes of the offenders might sometimes find it hard to swallow that they were not to punish offenders for anything they might have done in the past or might be planning in the future. But many officers who felt this way did not last as prison workers.

WEEK TWO

The second week of the mandatory prison work training taught us about pat-downs, cell searches, and contraband. During training, we were brought to a minimum-security prison to complete our own pat-downs and cell searches.

Pat-downs are completed face to face, so as I learned about them, I gained some insight when visitors came to the prison. I could now tell, observing pat-downs in progress, who had been through the experience before. Those who hadn't always turned around so that their backs were facing the officer, but the pros would stay facing front. During prison pat-downs, the men lined up to be patted down, and then we searched their cells.

As I learned how to pat down offenders, I and a uniformed female officer also going through the training had a bit of a different experience from the male officers. All the men wanted to come to us to be patted down. As soon as I finished one pat-down, the next man was volunteering. I didn't know if anyone else noticed this, but I most certainly did. The men weren't rude, but they had no problem spreading their legs and offering to tell me exactly where to pat them down. I respectfully told them thank you, but I didn't need their help.

During this shakedown, the security department at the prison we were visiting was looking for drugs. They had had a tip that new drugs might have recently been brought in. It was a minimum-security prison, and inmates went out to work for the day and had opportunities to bring in things. As we completed the shakedown, we wore gloves to search everything.

We went through pictures, opened heating ducts, looked in toilets, looked at bars of soap to make sure nothing was carved out of them, looked down bedposts, and inside all of the offenders' books. We took all the sheets off the beds. During one cell search, I inadvertently dumped someone's half-filled soda pop can all over his bed. I had to report the incident, and when the man came in, I apologized for the accident. He was cool with it.

Some of the men's cells were immaculate, while others were disgusting. Some had soiled underwear on the floors; old food opened on their shelves; or old, moldy lemonade still in their mugs.

Over the course of the week, the training instructors showed us all kinds of items considered contraband. We saw toothbrushes made to look like spears, handmade pistols that actually worked, long knives, screwdrivers, plastic shanks, pen shanks, sandpaper, balloons filled with dope, and socks filled with rocks. Offenders would steal from their jobs in the kitchen, woodworking, or laundry areas—anything that could be used to make a shank. Most just wanted protection for themselves. The offenders have hours upon hours to think, and they are very clever. They could encourage visitors to bring drugs in through creative means, perhaps by wrapping them in babies' diapers. I heard rumors of offenders that would stick drugs up their anus or swallow balloons with drugs or even flash drives in them. Then they would vomit up the goods when back in their cells. Once, I learned a man was found with three tins of chew up his anus. I wondered if the officer who told me that one was just playing with me. I found myself asking over and over, "How is all of this even possible?"

WEEK THREE

As training progressed, things got more and more hands on. During the third week, we learned about the prison's radio system and calling for help. We did an activity where we were set up in two teams of four and had to draw something communicated to us through the radio.

Each team received one radio and a set of precise instructions. Our challenge was to figure out which drawing the other team was looking at. It was like a map that we were drawing, and we were given specific directions from the other team to follow and help lead us to them.

Whoever had the radio could ask a couple of questions of the other team, but the person on the other end could answer only yes or no. The security warden, after an unknown, discretionary amount of time, handed the radio to the next person and gave more directions. The roles were reversed. Now, the other team asked questions to clarify what the first team had already asked, and the first team could only answer yes or no.

This went on for a while. Eventually it was my turn, and the security warden gave the radio to me. I knew I could ask any questions I wanted, and the person on the other end could ask what they wanted too. But we had to be aware that anyone could be listening. We had to draw the figure exactly as we believed it was situated, from exactly the same perspective as the other team. I noticed that the security warden watched this entire process. She went back and forth in both rooms and listened to and observed everyone. Other trainers were doing the same thing. I didn't realize it at the time, but we were being trained for a crisis. We had to pretend, on one end, that we were an officer and that on the other end was a captain. "Yes, Captain, understood." We kept both questions and answers short and to the point. We were to say as little as necessary while thinking and directing everyone as to where we were located.

We also learned how to properly hit the lifesaving button on our radios. The trainers instructed us to give our location and some details before hitting the button. We then had to wait five seconds before speaking once we hit the button. Although our location was given immediately and security could find us on camera, the things we said before we hit the button were supposed to inform officers and CERT teams where to start heading. We were to keep off the radios as much as possible because they were the primary means of communication the prisons used to convey critical information.

We learned to relay messages like, "This is Carson in the school. Officer needs help. Offender fighting an officer. We are in the Programs building, classroom one." Short, to-the-point communications over the radio could save lives, and we practiced them over and over.

We also watched a film of a robbery in progress. Security asked us to write down exactly what we saw. It was an eye-opener. Some people saw a black man although the man was actually white. Others said he was tall and stocky when he was in reality skinny. Some said he was wearing a white T-shirt, jeans, and tennis shoes. Others said he was wearing a face mask. Over the weeks, the training officers showed us video after video like this, or of other scenarios, and we became more and more observant each week.

We watched videos of fights and looked for shanks on inmates. We looked at mistakes employees made by not being observant, allowing offenders to listen to their conversations and thus learn about them and other staff.

We learned much about the inmates' con games and how each offender played a role in them. One would be the lookout, another would befriend you, another would act like they were going to hurt you, and the one that befriended you offered to keep you safe. This resulted in eventually convincing the "victim" that they needed to return the favor.

The men wanted drugs, phones, food, shanks and whatever they could get people to bring in for them. I heard that flash drives with pornography could go for about $250 to $400, if you could get hold of one—sometimes even more than that. The men learned how to hook them up to their televisions to watch. The more an offender had to offer, the higher the status he held.

WEEK FOUR

During the fourth week of training, we focused on handcuffs, shackles, and self-defense. We went over the proper way to handcuff a person and how the keyhole needed to face out, not in. If handcuffs were put on improperly, it would take more time to get them off. Offenders would get irritated while you messed with the key if their handcuffs were put on the wrong way. You could get kneed.

We had a plate to slide over the cuffs so the locks couldn't be picked. Supposedly, this plate had actually been designed by an inmate at another prison, and he made a huge amount of money off of his invention after leaving prison.

We also learned how to put on full-body restraints in the proper way so as to not get kneed or caught off guard. We trained in a multitude of positions, as the person holding down the offender and the person applying the restraints. After doing this for a couple hours, we had to show the trainers we all had the procedure and the positions down correctly. We learned to give offenders orders as we applied restraints: "Put your hands behind your back, palms up, legs only slightly spread." We were to be calm and respectful yet use a tone that was understood.

BRUISED RIBS

The self-defense training we learned in the system's mandatory course was intense. It was two full days of literally getting beat up. The instructors told us to take the training seriously enough to learn what we needed to know to protect ourselves but to be careful not to get hurt. My partner, Richard, another teacher from a different location, was tall and stocky, similar to me. I had to flip him over my back and put him on the floor, over and over again. He put me in a headlock, and I did the same to him. We fought cheek to cheek, shoulder to shoulder, with sweat pouring down our faces. The goal was for us to fight, even when we were tired, because we might need to do that someday to save our own lives or the lives of other prison employees.

We had to have a feel for both physical and mental exhaustion and yet keep moving. We couldn't be weak. We had to save our lives. We learned all the pain pressure points and were tested on them. We completed takedown after takedown. We got out of chokes. We brought each other down to our knees. We rolled across the mats, fighting to be free. We had others unexpectedly come up behind us while we were being distracted, and we had to react according to our training. If they went for a choke, we had to get our chins down and get out of the hold quickly. We learned if we got choked out, we could easily be raped and/or killed. We had to fight for our survival.

Fight. Survive. The instructors drilled it into our heads. The last time I flipped Richard over, I fell, and he came down on me. I heard my ribs pop. He heard the pop too. I ended up having them looked at by a doctor, and I suffered a lot of pain for the rest of the week. Luckily, my ribs were only bruised. That wasn't too bad. But my arms and face were bruised. People outside my job started asking me if I were being abused.

It was the most intense yet best educational training I have ever had. We learned to yell out orders: "Get down, now! I said, get down!" We held defense mats in front of our faces as we were kicking, punching, and yelling out orders all day. Richard said to me when we were done that he wouldn't want to go up against me in a fight. He shook my hand and said he was surprised with my strength, aggression, and attitude. We were told to think about these moves and be aware of our surroundings. When I went to class at the prison, I was to have my desk set up so that I could get out quickly if necessary. This meant that there had to be no chairs between the exits and me. As physical training ended, I felt stronger and more prepared for incidents that might arise at the prison.

K9 Training

We also trained with K9 units. A few CERT team members took our team across the road and discussed how to handle interactions with them and the dogs.

The instructors told us to walk past K9 officers on the side opposite the dog and not to make eye contact with the dog. If we were behind the dog and officer, we were supposed to stay back or let them know we were coming up from behind. We talked about how different dogs are trained to detect different contraband, like drugs and cigarettes. We were also given the opportunity to have a dog attack us. We put on dog-training arm vests, and the K9 officers told their dogs to attack. It was unbelievable how strong the dogs were. I almost got knocked to the ground! I learned that the officer hadn't even commanded the dog training with me to use full force. K9 dogs are very well-trained. It was a comfort to me afterward to see them with their masters in the yard.

Mace Use in Prisons

One optional training session the prison offered was mace use. I chose not to attend training to use mace. There was another session I was required to attend that was held that same day. The officers told me that if I ever decided I wanted to carry mace with me at the prison, I would be required to attend a mace-training session, which would include live training on how to react when sprayed in the face.

Mace use is a common method for breaking up fights in prison. Offenders are always warned before they are maced.

Later on in my time in the Walls, there was a fight down the hall from my classroom where two people were maced. I remember it vividly. It was 10:55 a.m. My students were coming to class. There was a lot of commotion as men entered the yard, library, barbershop, card room, and school, all while the counselor was conducting a class down at the end of the hallway. I had stepped out of my classroom to use the employee restroom directly across from my classroom when the radio alarm went off.

"We have a fight in the educational wing of the program's building." I quickly stepped back out of the restroom and looked down the hall. I saw a white man and a black man fighting. Right away, I wondered if it was gang related. I could hear the officers yell, "Get down on your knees. I am not going to tell you again. Get down." Then I heard the sound of the mace spraying out from its container. I exited the hallway, stepping back into my classroom and instantly started coughing. I can still remember how it felt. As the fight ended, the two men, one of whom was May, one of my students, were shackled and taken out. I could not stop coughing for over an hour from the fumes of the mace, but the students weren't affected at all. Officer Dan took Shorty, another of my students, to look through storage to see if they could find a fan for me. I couldn't teach because I couldn't stop coughing, and so the men worked together on the assignment, and Shorty worked out some problems on the board. The special education teacher, Troy, was in the room next door. He was a man in his sixties who was semiretired. He had COPD (chronic obstructive pulmonary disease). When I saw him, his face was bright red, and he was holding his inhaler, struggling to breathe. I called Officer Dan, who came and took him out. There are a couple golf carts to get around the prison grounds with, and Officer Dan gave Troy a ride to the main building because he couldn't walk. Once Troy was out of the building and breathing fresh air, he recovered quite quickly, but he did not come back into the building that day. It stuck with me how not one of the students coughed, not a flinch or a throat clearing. They just kept on going like it was a normal day. I reflected about how different the worlds from which we came are. In their world, people could get used to the effects of mace and become indifferent to the sounds of fighting.

Teacher Plans

Throughout the few years I worked in the prison, I attended more self-defense trainings and other informative trainings, including first aid classes. I received required hepatitis vaccinations and was checked yearly for tuberculosis, which along with HIV and hepatitis were among the most common diseases affecting prison inmates.

During the weeks I attended the required training courses, every night I reflected on what I had learned. To this day, I am aware of my surroundings and always know where the exit doors are no matter what room I am in. Even now, I pay closer attention to my current students and the outside environment, and I do not like having my back to others.

Each night I would study for the weekly training test, and as I did, I found myself using the time to start planning my strategy for teaching my new students. After a few more months of training, I would be their only teacher, and I wanted them to learn from me.

During the few weeks at the prison before my training, I had observed my new students very carefully. I looked in their files to see what educational levels they each had reached. I got a feel for how serious each was about school and learning. The majority didn't have a goal other than to get paid. That needed to change. I wanted to get more students attending school. I wanted to make the prison school a place where learning happened, where the students came to work and not to talk or listen to music.

Through the weeks of training, I learned that the absolute best way to protect myself was to get my students engaged, to inspire them to care about themselves and others and show them how education could change their lifestyle and their outlook. I would get a whiteboard for math, I decided, and begin working on my students' language. The way people talk influences the way that they think and feel. So, I thought, no more gang references. No more foul language. I didn't want to hear any more "homies," "homeboys," fucks, shits, double negatives, or can'ts. We would start with language, and eventually, all my students would pass a writing test. These would be my first two changes to the prison school when I returned from training. From there, we would work on confidence, teamwork, listening, and everything else that came with learning. As I learned, I planned ahead. I couldn't wait to get back and put all my plans into action.

4

Disciplinary Reports and Progress Reports

Success does not consist in never making mistakes
but in never making the same one a second time.
—George Bernard Shaw

On my first day back in the Walls after my leave for mandatory train-ing, I was still a bit bruised and battered from my experiences in the self-defense course. As I took the long walk down the sidewalk to the prison, my mind was on all the things I had learned over the past month. I had spent the last weeks of the training excited, planning ahead for the new lessons and policies I intended to implement in the classroom, but now, as I returned to work, I was wary. I had a fresh awareness of my circumstances and surroundings, and, as I had been taught, I began to project out worst-case scenarios that could occur inside the prison. If I were grabbed from behind, how would I stop a man from choking me out? If someone came at me from the front, how would I defend myself long enough for officers to reach me? If a student got extremely upset, how could I de-escalate the situation? Would the men try con games on me?

Despite how all this might sound, I wasn't afraid on that first morn-ing when I returned to work. But the training had done its job. I was no longer naive to what could potentially happen. I was more prepared. But the kind of heightened awareness I had been taught through my training courses was a different kind of behavior for me, one that I had had to learn, and I wasn't totally comfortable with it yet.

I passed through the metal detector and into the prison, walked upstairs, and unlocked my assigned set of keys. It hit me that I was walking into the Walls alone for the first time. Now that I had completed the training, I would no longer have to rely on an escort as I walked throughout the prison. As I thought of that, my chief source of nervousness was not the men or their behavior toward myself but whether I could find my way through the maze to Door Seven.

The officer set my radio in the door box and slid it over to me. As I reached to pick it up, once again everything I had learned in the training courses passed through my head, and I remembered that the radio was now my lifeline. I turned it on, gazing at the red button on it, clipped it to my waist, and continued my long journey to Door Seven. There, the men welcomed me back, and once again, they were my students, with smiles on their faces and ready to chatter.

Now the primary teacher in the school, over the next couple of weeks, I learned more about my students and the tutors I had inherited. They all loved to talk, especially to people living in the free world. I knew most of the men had televisions in their cells, yet I was pleasantly surprised with how knowledgeable they were on world news. My students all listened to the news daily, and politics was always a big discussion topic in our classroom. In fact, these major offenders, incarcerated in a high-security prison, knew more about world events than most civilians I knew outside. They could converse intelligently about anything and everything happening on the other side of the walls. While I did wonder how much of the news they had kept up with when they lived on the outside, as I talked with them, I also remember thinking, *How sad that these men can't vote.*

Of course, their favorite political topic was justice reform. It gave them hope. The justice reform movement is gaining strength in our nation today, and during my time in the Walls, even the lifers were beginning to believe that if they made changes in their behavior, some-day, they might be given a second chance.

A Hope for Second Chances

There are almost 2.3 million people in the United States criminal jus-tice system.[1] Our country is the not-so-proud holder of the title of the nation with the most people incarcerated per capita on Earth. Many are imprisoned for nonviolent offenses. Some inmates I have personally worked with are incarcerated for murder when they were merely pres-ent at the time the gun was fired. Conditions in correctional facilities can be dire, and while there are occasionally therapists and courses available to help offenders cope with anger and mental health issues, resources are often scarce, and many prisons today remain glorified holding pens, with little to no focus on rehabilitating inmates to rejoin society.

This is changing. There is a growing movement to change the United States justice system for the better. In 2018, Congress passed the First Step Act, including key portions of the Sentencing Reform and Corrections Act, which was introduced in 2015 and failed to pass in 2016. The new act's passage demonstrates the increasing bipartisan push for reducing mass incarceration. The First Step Act focuses on improving conditions in federal prisons and reorienting prisons around rehabilitation. Vocational training, educational classes, and behavioral therapy for all participants is on the rise, and credits in these programs may allow for earlier release.

Although my students understood why many oppose justice reform in our society, they loved talking about all the influential people helping

1. Wendy Sawyer and Peter Wagner, Prison Policy Initiative, "Mass Incarceration: The Whole Pie 2020," press release, March 24,2020, https://www.prisonpolicy.org/reports/pie2020.html.

to make positive changes to our penal system. They shared how, for many years, they had just existed, going on with their daily routines of eating, working, watching television, and exercising, waiting for the day they would die. But now, with grassroots movements, activists, certain politicians, and other influential individuals working on their side, they had hope for change in the future.

Some of the inmates wished these leaders would come talk to them, so they could help them understand life on the inside. Over their years in prison, the inmates had had a lot of time to think, and all that thinking had evolved into positive ideas they wanted to share. I told them that by improving their writing skills, they could take the first step and write to leaders in the justice reform movement to invite them to visit or just write them a simple thank-you for their efforts.

Of course, their first response was, "Those people would never read our letters. They wouldn't listen to us."

I replied, "How do you know until you try?"

As the men spent more time with me in school, I worked on changing their negative thinking. I emphasized a can-do attitude. "We are not going to use *can't* anymore," I told them. "We will be positive and learn how to use that positivity in good ways." I believed this would help them earn the second chances they craved, or at the very least the opportunity to make a bigger difference in the prison itself, as leaders in the community inside, tutors in the school, members on a board to make improvements, or speakers when tours came to visit. Even responsibilities such as this can give offenders pride and purpose.

In my time in the Walls, I came to believe in the need for prison reform. Not all offenders do, but many gain a structure through the rules of prison life. They may learn teamwork, how to work a job, punctuality, and respect for others. These qualities were missing from their lives on the outside. Unfortunately, due to our current laws, many offenders who may have the opportunity to become better, more stable people in prisons never get the chance to use their newfound skills outside of the walls. It's a twisted irony: we educate and give them the skills they were missing on the outside, only to never let them out to use them.

But things were changing for my students as they changed for offenders across the nation. The two inmate-tutors with whom I began working knew all about second chances. They had originally been given life sentences without parole. However, with the new changes to juvenile sentencing, their sentences had been changed to life *with* parole. This was a very big deal to them. Now, there was a real possibility that perhaps they wouldn't leave prison in a body bag. It gave them the drive to move forward.

SHOOTER

My first inmate-tutor, Shooter, had earned a life sentence for kidnaping and rape at the age of sixteen. He was a juvenile, under the age of eighteen, when he committed this crime. When I met him, he had been in prison for approximately sixteen years.

For most of his time in prison, Shooter had been a model inmate, but when he and I first became acquainted, he had recently broken his record. He explained to me, "I may not be at the school long. I just want you to know that. I have to go before the judge because I got in some trouble. It's my own fault. I was running a little gambling business, and I got caught. I did it, and I'm going to tell the judge that I did it. I haven't been in trouble in a very long time, and I know better. It was more out of boredom than anything else."

Shooter was from El Salvador, and if he were ever paroled under the new juvenile sentencing laws, he would be sent back there. He doesn't know El Salvador. He has spent most of his life within the United States. But he said that if he were ever given that precious second chance, he would gladly return to the country of his birth.

Shooter did not end up going to lockup for his gambling offense. The judge respected his honesty and the fact that he acknowledged his wrongdoing, did not make excuses, and hadn't been in any trouble for the previous sixteen years. He returned to the school and remained an excellent tutor. I still keep in contact with him today.

SUGAR

When I began working at the prison, Sugar, a twenty-three-year-old white man, was the other inmate-tutor. At the age of seventeen, he had been sentenced to die in prison. He killed two family members, execution style. He had planned the killings and even researched how to protect his ears from the sound of the gun firing. He said he was abused and that led up to the murders. He knew me well enough to know that I would not feel sorry for him, and I told him I did not. There are people who would have been willing to help him, and there were other ways to handle bad situations without hurting someone else.

Sugar was brilliant; he had book smarts. He had completed the schooling program quickly with high scores that had earned him his place as a tutor. Again, because of the change in the law, his sentence had been altered. He had a possibility of parole and of getting out someday.

Unfortunately, Sugar did not last long as a tutor. I heard that he was caught engaging in sexual misconduct with another offender. In any event, he was sent to lockup for some time. Because he had been in lockup before, he was not accepted back as a tutor. When you are in the hole for that length of time, school continues without you—with tutors who can be present.

WHEELS

During my time in the Walls, I didn't lose only tutors to misconduct. Sometimes I lost my students too.

Even before Wheels entered my classroom, I knew he was a rule breaker who had spent time in the hole. Officer Dan had already told me he wouldn't be in school long.

"As soon as he gets out of the hole, he goes right back in," Dan said. "He's been in school forever and has yet to earn a diploma or even pass a test."

He told me how, for five years, Wheels, a large black man who probably tipped the scale at three hundred pounds, "walked" everywhere around the prison on his knees, complaining of back pain. He actually started tying his shoes to his knees and moving around like that. I can only imagine how uncomfortable he must have felt. He needed a wheelchair, he insisted. But after the officers watched him walking around his cell every day, relaxing and showing no signs of pain, they ignored his request.

Finally, Officer Dan said, "Wheels, aren't you sick of this? You'd move so much faster if you would walk. And don't tell me you can't because we watch you every day. As soon as you get in your cell, you're on your feet. I am sick of it, so knock it the fuck off."

Because Officer Dan had always showed him respect, Wheels listened, and from then on, he walked like everyone else. I'm not sure how Dan got through to him, but maybe Wheels just needed to know someone noticed and cared.

The day we met, I sat down next to him to help him with math, and he said, "I got plans, Miss Beth. I am goin' to New York to be a DJ. I'm going to take you with me and make millions. We are going to live the high life."

I looked directly in his eyes. "That will never happen, so get it out of your head now. I'm not going anywhere with you, and if I hear you talk like this again, I'll write you up." I was straight with him. I knew that was what he needed to hear. "You are not making millions of dollars as a DJ," I told him. "This world has changed so much since you came in. It's great to have goals, but millions? Work on getting educated, and then you can talk about your DJ dreams."

The next day, Wheels was out in the corridor, pounding on Door Seven. I was on my break, and no students were at school at the time.

"Miss Beth," he said, "I have a pass to see you. Open the door." He kept banging at the door. "Let me in!"

Officer Dan had been right to warn me to watch out for him.

"I'm not opening the door for you," I replied. "You don't belong here. Who gave you a pass?"

"The officer in my pod."

The steel door between us was not only locked but too heavy for him to get open, so I knew he wasn't able to get near me. As he pounded at the door, I wasn't afraid. But I was very, very aware. I called down to Officer Tate in the chapel because he was also my officer at the time. I explained that Wheels was banging on the door and asking to enter. Officer Tate came right up and sent Wheels back to his unit, calling ahead to inform the officers in his unit about what had just happened. Wheels knew he wasn't allowed at the school. It turned out that the officer who had written the pass thought he was going to the chapel because he was assigned to work there.

Wheels told Officer Tate he was just stopping in to say hi. Nobody believed that one. I certainly didn't. Because of the incident, Wheels lost his job at the chapel. He went back to Unit One and was told he could only come down the hall for his hour of school.

His behavior didn't improve much after that. When in school, he would continually stare at me. I finally had enough and told him if he stared at me one more time, I would write him up. "I've had enough," I said, "and you need to find something better to look at."

That did it for him. Once again, he had just needed to be put in his place, and I never caught him staring at me again. But he never did take school seriously. He read through all the lessons. I finally had to give him an ultimatum—improve, or I won't allow you back in. Wheels went to lockup again shortly after, and I didn't see him again.

During the early part of my time in the Walls, I had repeat incidents like this one of students not committing to education or self-improvement. The shift to managed enrollment, where students came to actual classes and attendance was required, improved our ability to make the prison school more than a way for the offenders to pass the time or a job for them to work. Over time, the vision I had worked out in training of what the school could be became more and more of a reality.

The other teacher and I discussed how we would teach real classes instead of handing out worksheets, functioning as glorified tutors. I would teach math, and she would teach writing. She also wanted to get moving toward managed enrollment. We were due to move to a newly built prison soon, and the other teacher would be taking on a new position in the education department. She wanted the new school system up and running by the time we were settled at the new prison. It was the perfect time to make changes, with a new working classroom, a new program, and new hope for all those without an education.

SHORTY

When I returned from training, I saw that a few new students had shown up in my classroom. Some previous students had gone to lockup, and others moved to different units. One of the offenders who moved up was Shorty. He was no longer in Unit One, so he could attend school all day (other than at count time and when Unit One was at school). In the beginning, his English was very broken, and I struggled to understand him. But he worked hard and read every day. Soon, I noticed positive changes in his speech. At this point, he had been in school for more than ten years with no success. I heard through the grapevine that he came to school to keep an eye on everyone, and it was rumored that he was a very powerful gang leader. That didn't bother me, and I never saw any signs of it, so it didn't matter, rumor or not. However, I made it crystal clear that if he were to attend school, it was with the understanding that he would learn English and graduate. He knew I was serious because the men who preceded him shared that my school was all about learning, not socializing.

As I walked around the room, answering questions and discussing subject areas, I constantly asked the men if they needed help. Once they knew I meant business, they worked hard, and Shorty actually got excited about taking the math class. Before I left for the mandatory training, I had told the men I intended to start teaching a couple of math classes upon my return to school. They did not forget this. Indeed, Shorty took it upon himself to find a whiteboard for me to use. Shorty liked everything clean. When he moved units to spend more time in school, he took it upon himself to wipe down tables and sweep. He found a whiteboard in the room where the broom was kept. He carefully placed two chairs at the front of the classroom and set the board on them. Then he had the men move the tables in the room so that the area was more conducive to learning.

These men are ready, I thought, when I saw what they had done.

As with the majority of my students, Shorty's vocabulary initially consisted of words I did not appreciate hearing in the classroom. But I did not back down on the resolve I had made in training, and over the months, Shorty, along with the rest of my students, began using more appropriate language as time went on, another point on which I would not back down.

When I began teaching my planned math classes, I really pushed the men. We worked hard every day, and they went back to their cells with folders containing homework. Shorty would get mad at me and complain that I was crazy and pushing him too hard. He kept saying that he couldn't do the math because it was much too hard for him. We discussed a solution. Apparently, he needed more time to study above and beyond school to keep up with the classwork. Since I was not going to change the pace of the class, I explained that I expected the men would make adjustments in their after-school activities to make sure they were keeping up. But this was part of the learning process: giving up something to gain something more valuable and beneficial. It wasn't so much about needing to go at a given pace but more about teaching them that life can be challenging, and instead of giving up, they needed to find a solution—or create one out of thin air, if necessary.

"What do you spend time doing outside of class?" I asked Shorty.

"Work on my case," he said. "Lift weights, play handball and soccer, watch TV, especially my soaps."

Now that he was out of Unit One, he worked in the kitchen. Unit One offenders were not allowed to work. If the offenders attended school, they weren't required to work, even though many did for the money. Shorty was a baker, and so he went to work at four o'clock in the morning to prepare the bread and desserts for the day.

"Let's try a compromise," I said. "Sometimes, you need to give up things to accomplish your goals. You can continue to work out, play soccer, and watch the news, okay? But until school is over, no more soap operas. Spend that time solving math problems."

He looked shocked, but I could see that he understood I wasn't scared of him and didn't pity him.

"It's going to be hard," he said, "but I'll do it."

When he said that, I knew he respected me.

In the next few months, he spent many hours working on his English, and he improved immensely. When math class was over, some men stayed and worked on other subjects or math while others went back to their cells. Shorty always stayed and worked.

Over time, he told me a little about his family. His girlfriend had been pregnant with his son when his life changed for the worse and he was incarcerated. But even then, Shorty had helped raise his son from behind prison bars. His determination to be an involved parent had paid off, and he had a close bond with his son.

One day, as I sat at a round table, discussing math with him and another offender, Shorty mentioned that he had told his son he was taking a math class. His son had replied that he was taking an algebra class and struggling with it.

"So," Shorty asked me, "what is algebra? I don't want him to know that I don't know this math. I don't want him to think I'm dumb."

We discussed it, and Shorty said he had encouraged his son to keep working and to ask for help.

"This is an opportunity to help my son," he told me. "I have to learn this algebra."

His son was the catalyst he needed to work harder and give up even more outside activities to accomplish this new goal. In Math 1, he was learning about fractions, percentages, and decimals. The class would eventually progress to basic algebra. I explained to him that my Math 2 class was doing more advanced algebra. So, while I was teaching Math 2, he sat in the back of the room, working on his Math 1. But he also took notes for Math 2. He spent the entire day in school focusing on math, which soon made it possible for him to join the Math 2 class.

Shooter, the tutor I mentioned earlier, told me the offenders made fun of Shorty because he carried his books with him everywhere he went and was studying all the time. I was proud of him! He didn't care in the least that others made fun of him. He was enjoying this new world of learning. And he could handle himself.

When Shorty joined the Math 2 class, he sat right up front. I noticed that every time I went to erase the board, he jumped up and said, "I'll do it." If I dropped something, he'd hurry to pick it up. He did so not only to be polite but because the men enjoyed staring at my butt when I turned around or bent over. Although they got mad at him for taking away their fun, he did it anyway. This was his way of showing me appreciation and respect. Although I wasn't asking for any favors and never thanked him, I did notice his efforts and was quietly grateful.

A Class to Remember

I particularly enjoyed teaching that first Math 2 class. Besides Shorty, the four other men in the class included Jons, Burt, Mars, and Robs. After a few weeks with them, I felt Jons would have the best chance of passing the first round of testing. He was young and hadn't been out of school very long, so math was still somewhat fresh in his mind. He became something of a test case for me. I knew it was important for the men to see someone succeed, to see someone could pass the math test. If Jons passed and the others didn't, they would keep working, aware the test could be passed. If Jons and all the others failed their first attempt, I would have to really struggle to keep them motivated.

Burt sat on the front row with Jons and Shorty. He was a black man with a life sentence. Like many of my students, he had committed a gang-related crime. He had been caught during his initiation, randomly shooting a man to join a gang. He had simply picked someone on the street—a man walking to a video store with his fiancée to rent a movie—and shot him. Burt was now in his forties and had been in school at the prison for a while, but he hadn't passed any tests. When Shorty joined the Math 2 class early, Burt seemed jealous. He felt Shorty should have to wait until the next round. But his competitiveness with Shorty motivated him to work harder, and at any rate, Burt did not make the decisions about who was ready to work on which level. I did. No student was going to be held back if he had the potential and work ethic to move forward.

At times, Burt's frustration got the best of him. He would get really mad at me if he didn't understand something. He wanted an explanation the instant he hit any road block, and if I was helping another student, it really bothered him. His legs would start twitching or moving, and he would put his head between his hands as he sat waiting for my attention. Many times, Burt would need to get up and just pace the room to let out some stress.

The Math 2 class was intense. He hadn't seen much of this math in a very long time. A couple of times I had to send Burt back to his cell because he couldn't control his anger, but I avoided calling him out in front of the others.

Burt was a good student. He always had all his assignments completed and more. So whenever I saw him begin to get worked up, I would say, "Burt, you have worked really hard today, you're ahead, and so why don't you take a break from class today? If you do too much math, you're going to get burnt out. You'll get your pay today because you already completed all the work, so don't worry about that. Just go back and relax."

He would listen and head back to his cell. He would come back the next day ready to work and always apologized for his behavior, and it wasn't often that things got so bad in the first place. I recall having to send Burt back to his cell only three times, and the other men never commented on it. Everyone had their frustrations.

I told all the men that I understood their frustrations with the math. I had set a rigorous pace, and everyone had to work hard to keep up. Whenever things became too much, I encouraged my students to get up and move around the room, to step away from the problem for a moment.

I have come across many people who seem to think earning the GED or High School Equivalency Diploma (HSED) is easy. It is not. To pass the math test, you need to understand algebra, geometry, and advanced algebra, which can be difficult for offenders who have had interrupted or incomplete educations, who may not speak English well, or may have spent many years away from a school environment.

However, with hard work and perseverance, anything is possible. When our Math 2 class began, the men sat and worked by themselves. They only ever asked me questions. As we progressed, however, they began opening up to each other and working more as a team. They were breaking barriers and feeling comfortable as a class. When the "fences come down," as a colleague of mine likes to say, learning picks up momentum. Students start to ask more questions, focus less on time concerns, laugh, discuss, show creativity and uniqueness, and begin thinking, sounding, and looking like a team. This is when they are confident and no longer scared to make mistakes.

Mars and Robs sat behind Burt, Jons, and Shorty. Mars was a short, stocky black man with dreads serving a life sentence. When I became his teacher, he had three tests left to complete, and he was confident he would pass the math test.

Mars started out as the class clown. One day, I felt I needed to have a discussion with him. "You need to get serious, Mars," I told him.

He looked confused and told me he was serious. I don't think he realized how loud he was being.

"I'm actually excited to come to real class," he assured me. From that point on, as the other men got deeper into math, Mars got quieter. He understood how important it was for all the students to remain focused.

Later, I heard that Mars's sentence was being brought back to trial, so I asked him if he had any future plans. He told me he wanted to attend culinary school in Illinois when he completed his sentence. So, when he came in the next day for class, I handed him a folder with everything he needed to know about the college and coursework for a career in the culinary field. We talked about all the classes he would need to take, which included some math. He was surprised and grateful, and after that, he was no longer working simply in a better classroom environment; he was working toward a purpose.

Robs was a white man with glasses and long sandy-blond hair that he frequently wore in a ponytail. He was in his early thirties. His current prison term was his second time in the pen, but soon he would be out, and I needed to make sure he was prepared. I did not want him returning. A simple man, Robs was in for fraud. He had written some bad checks after an inheritance his "friends" absorbed. He bought his friends whatever they wanted and just kept writing checks even after he was out of money. I think he loved the attention he received by gifting to the people he called friends. Once he served his time for this, he got in some more trouble and punched an officer in the face. This really surprised me because he was always calm, kind, and respectful to me.

Robs was a sensitive man. In class one day, another inmate made a comment about his long hair, saying that he needed to cut it. Robs just put his head down, and I knew the comment had hurt him.

I looked at my students. "What's wrong with long hair?" I asked them. "I have long hair, and I happen to like it." I looked over at Robs, and he grinned.

The next day he came to class without a ponytail, just his long hair hanging down and a smile on his face.

Robs had been in school for some time, and now that he had time constraints, we needed to work on math all day. He was a good reader and enjoyed history, so his last test didn't concern me. What did was the fact that, in the previous year, he had tried passing the math test twice and failed. He had only one more shot at it. This put pressure on both of us.

He and Shorty became math partners, working nonstop all day. As the class came together as a team, the other students in Math 2 pushed him and laughed with him, doing their best to help him relax. We all wanted Robs to receive his diploma as much as he wanted to get it.

The five men in Math 2 worked hard, keeping their eyes on the concepts at hand, and, of course, outside of regularly scheduled classes, I stayed busy in other ways. I was always available to work with my students one on one on math or on any subject with which they needed help.

THE GREAT COPY MACHINE CAPER

Not that my students were always so focused on their studies. We were making headway in my pupils' studies and in their character development, but I never forgot that this was a prison classroom. The training I had gone through was always in my head, reminding me to stay alert and observant. On my long walk in each morning, I continued to think about self-defense strategies and project out hypothetical worst-case scenarios, not to scare myself but to ensure I was prepared for what could happen each day.

I was never involved in any violent altercations or hostage situations during my time in the Walls, but my training did one day enable me to recognize a situation in progress. I had a student named Roster who one day decided that he would make some copies on the decrepit copy machine in my classroom. The machine was located next to the entrance of the room where Troy worked part time and where the cages were located.

Roster knew only tutors were allowed to use the copy machine, but that didn't stop him. As I sat with my back to the machine, I noticed a couple of the men looking behind me. When I turned around, I saw Roster opening up the machine. My tutor, Shooter, was beside him, and they seemed to be dealing with a paper jam.

"I was just trying to help Shooter fix the jammed printer," Roster insisted.

I wasn't buying it. I walked over to the machine and took a look at what he'd been trying to copy—graphic pornography pictures drawn by one of the offenders.

"I'm going to have to call Officer Tate and report it," I told Roster.

He begged me not to, but, in my eyes, that was just another test. And I was going to pass.

When the officer came upstairs, I explained to him what had happened and showed him the photos. He called on the radio and requested a couple CERT members, who came and took Roster to lockup. This would be the first of two major reports I wrote.

I continued with class, even though I could hear the men talking about how my face had turned red. They thought I had been embarrassed by the pornography. I knew I needed to set the record straight, but I chose not to that particular day. Instead, I gave my response to the incident at the end of the Math 2 class so what I said would travel around the entire yard.

I stood at the front of the classroom and said, "I know you think the pornography incident yesterday embarrassed me. I heard you—by the way, I am not deaf. If you have something to say to me, be man enough to say it to me. My face turned red yesterday because I was ticked off, not because of the pornography. I was ticked off because Roster was trying to pull one over on me. Actually, you were all trying to pull one over on me. I'm not stupid; you knew what he was up to. You also knew the printer is off limits.

"I understand that many of you haven't been with a woman in some time, so pictures are it. But I came to the prison with no ill will toward anyone. I made no judgment calls. I only asked that you study and take school seriously to help yourselves, and I didn't ask for anything in return.

"I have purposely ignored all of your little muttering comments about my clothes, butt, or whatever else you say because, to me, they're childish. And I am hoping that, as we go along, you will grow in your education and maturity, and that immature talk will go away. I made it crystal clear that I am by the book. If you want to try to get away with something, that is your choice. But if I see something that is against the rules, I will report it—just as, if I see you are doing great, I will give you a positive generic note."

(A generic note is written to inform staff how the men are behaving. When offenders receive good generic notes, some like to give copies to their attorneys or parole boards. It is a record of how they are handling themselves in prison. When they come up for review each year, their generic notes are reviewed.)

I made eye contact with everyone in the room and concluded, "I am showing you respect, and I expect the same in return. This was a good lesson for everyone."

Shorty came up to me after class and told me I was right to write up Roster, but I was not going to be played by him either.

"Right or wrong," I said, "I'm not asking for your opinion. I don't want or need your approval for what I do."

I had to be stern. I appreciated what Shorty said. I could tell he meant it, but in a prison environment, it's important to maintain the power balance.

About a month after this incident, an officer who was walking out looked over and said, "Do you remember Roster, the young kid you reported for porn?"

I nodded, and the officer continued, "Thank you for not letting that go. Because of your report, we searched his entire cell and found gang stuff. We hadn't been aware of his affiliations, and he served extra time in lockup due to it." He smiled as he turned and headed to his vehicle, and I continued straight to mine.

Roster hadn't been at the prison very long. The officers now knew which gang he belonged to. The more security knew about these men, the better. It helped keep everyone safe.

After this incident, I felt I better understood the importance of keeping the men accountable. My actions had made a difference, and I kept up my vigilance throughout my time in the Walls.

Robs's Walk to Freedom

Although I was glad to have contributed to the safety of the prison, my joy continued to be in giving my students the education they lacked and opening the doors to their future.

As October turned around my first year in the prison, I began to focus hard on Robs in my Math 2 class. I was running out of time to help him understand this math. We had dates set and goals to meet. He needed to take a practice test at the end of November. He had until January to finish, and he needed time after passing the practice test to study for his upcoming official test in social studies.

He successfully passed his practice math test with me, but his solo attempt at the practice test was not successful. He failed by a single point. *One point, no big deal, he's got this*, I thought. It was okay. We still had a couple of weeks, and I wanted him to practice test so that he could relieve stress and see how fast he was progressing. We studied hard, and at the beginning of December, he passed the practice math test on his own. Now, it was time to take the official test.

I was concerned, even though I did not let Robs or the other men see how stressed I had become. I knew how important this test was for him. Unlike the others, who weren't getting out of prison anytime soon, this could make the difference as to whether Robs would be successful in the free world. In his heart, he believed his success depended on the test. I wanted him to leave prison with the confidence that he could make it outside, and I admit that I tossed and turned all night, worrying about what would happen the next morning.

Quietly, I walked into the prison, thinking only about Robs's testing. Were there some last words I could say to him to help boost him up? Should I just talk about other things? What if Robs wasn't feeling well? He needed to be confident and at his best. My mind was racing.

The tutors arrived at school before the students, so I pulled Sugar and Shooter aside and said, "Let's not talk about the test with Robs."

So, when the inmates arrived, Sugar started talking about birds. *Birds?* I thought. We could do better than that. Yet Sugar continued, rambling on about how so many little birds were outside sitting on a tree by the window. How could all these birds be here in December? It was a mild December because we had no snow. Others joined in, working as a team to relax Robs. Robs just sat at a table, listening. Good enough! He was nervous but still focused on the men's bizarre conversation.

An employee named Shannon came to give Robs his official math test. She pulled me to another room and said that she thought it would be a tough day for him.

"He's been trying for years to pass, and I'm not sure he's capable of this higher-level math," she told me. "I think he got lucky passing the official practice test."

I knew he struggled with math, but I had seen him learn a lot since I first met him. I remembered going over testing strategies and math drills that he didn't know before. He needed only a passing grade! He deserved a passing grade because he knew the math! Yes, it was harder for him than for others, but he was still capable, and only his anxiety was hurting him now.

I smiled at Shannon and spoke loudly enough for Robs to hear me. "Today is going to be a great day. He's got this. He will pass."

Shannon called Robs into the room to test, and the others patted him on the back and wished him luck. How far they had come from making fun of his long hair. We all waited patiently, if not anxiously, for him to test.

Jons asked me if I thought he would pass.

"Yes," Shooter said, before I could reply. "It is his time."

Shooter was right. Robs's days in prison were coming to an end, and he had to pass because he would never give himself this chance on the outside.

Robs had ninety minutes to complete the test, and he used every minute of it. I watched the clock, walking by the door frequently and glimpsing in at him. He couldn't see me because his back was to the door. When his time came to an end, I took another look into the room. Robs sat at the desk, his head in his hands, crying. Unaware that I was watching, he wiped the tears from his cheeks. Shannon brought him a tissue. He took it but didn't move for about five minutes. I was worried, but then he looked up and saw me staring at him.

As tears rushed down his face, he nodded his head. *Yes!*

I did everything to maintain my composure, filled with joy and pride. I waited for him to come out of the room, so he could tell the other men. Grinning, each one gave Robs a hug and shook his hand. He could now take his final test and graduate. That night, I shed tears.

Robs progressed to that final step. He passed his final test and earned his diploma, and when he left the prison, he entered the free world with an education. That was the one thing no one could steal from him, not even those "friends" of his who had helped him spend his inheritance.

After Robs completed his last test, he left school, but I asked him to stop in before leaving prison. I wanted to know where to send his diploma when it arrived and to talk about his future plans.

When Robs came to see, we talked for a long time. I knew where he was headed and that he had no family waiting for him. I looked up some halfway homes and places where he could look for work, along with a few activities in which he might want to participate. I knew his counselor had already given this material to him, but I wanted to review it with him and hear what he was thinking. I wanted him to tell me his plan when he stepped off the bus and onto the well-trod pavement in the outside world. Where would he walk? Who would be there to meet him?

He planned to walk to a halfway house we had talked about that wasn't far from the bus station. He said he had already been in contact with the director there, and they would help him find work. He thanked me and shook hands with the men, who wished him well.

Then, he gave me a hug, and tears filled his eyes.

"I'll be okay," he promised me. "I'll stay out of trouble."

As he exited Door Seven for the last time, Robs looked back, smiled, and continued on his way.

I locked the door behind him. Finally, I let my own tears flow as I watched him head back to his cell house for the last time on this new walk of freedom.

PRACTICE TESTS FOR EVERYONE

Robs wasn't the only one in Math 2 preparing to complete the unit, even though he was the first to test. We all continued to work, and time flew by. Finally, the day arrived when I would give the men my own practice test, where I would evaluate if they were ready for a practice test with an official test administrator.

They were quiet and nervous. Mars told me that he wasn't concerned because he knew he would pass, but the others voiced their doubts. Despite his words of confidence, I knew Mars was scared too. He just didn't want the men to know it.

Shorty told me I was crazy to believe he would ever pass. All the men looked and spoke as if they were both exhausted and defeated. I knew this was their way of covering the fear of failing in front of their classmates. I could feel how badly they wanted to pass the test and knew that they were hoping and praying to.

Making light of it, I said, "Remember, this is just a practice test. When you pass, we will move on to the official practice test in two days. Just take your time, rule out answers that don't make sense, and relax. It is just one test, and there will be many more." I never mentioned not passing the test because I wanted only positive words to go in their heads.

When they completed the practice exam, they wanted to know the results immediately and paced the room as I graded.

"Good news," I told them, and watched relief wash over every face. "You all passed."

No one could say they were smarter or better than the others. We didn't discuss scores, and surprisingly, no one thought to ask how many points they earned. They were all in shock, I suppose, so they went back to their units to relax for the rest of the day.

"Take a break," I told them. "Play some basketball, watch some television, or just chill, and tomorrow we will review." I even told Shorty he should go watch his favorite soap opera. And I finished by saying, "I had no doubt you would all pass." I did in fact have some doubt, not because of lack of knowledge but lack of confidence. Showing more confidence in class wasn't the same as sitting in front of an important test with no guidance. But they had done it.

They left with smiles on their faces, walking quickly and with a measure of pride on the way back to their units. Clearly, they were excited, but I knew they were also anxious about what was to come.

Unlike most of our intense days together, the next day in class, we didn't do much math. Instead, we talked about their progress and how proud I was that they hadn't given up. I asked them how they had spent the night before and how they had celebrated their success. I was surprised that none of them had shared the good news with their families back home. I realized that they still weren't confident about the real test, so they hadn't wanted to say anything just yet.

We laughed and joked, but Burt was ready to get back to work. I told him that he was ready and that we would study again once he passed the official practice test.

We had used some of our time together to talk, so I explained that they could go back and chill for the evening. "Get a good night's sleep because tomorrow is a big day for all of you," I said. "Please try to go to bed by nine o'clock because you will need to be here by nine tomorrow morning. Have a good breakfast, and I will see you then." That next morning, they all walked in together, and I could see the nervousness in each of them. "Well good morning, men," I said. "I hope you all were able to have a good breakfast this morning. Today is going to be an awesome day. Smile, relax, and just take the test."

I was prepared in case someone didn't pass the test. I would keep that student or students after class for a talk. Fortunately, all the men came out of the test room smiling. Every one of them had passed, earning a seat to take the official test to prove their math competency.

I told them, "We have a week to review before the official test. Go relax, and we'll get started tomorrow." I was so happy and excited for them, but I stayed direct and confident because I knew that we had not climbed to the top of the hill yet. We were only three-quarters of the way up. The big moment would be next week with the final exam.

That entire week we worked hard, and I would go home and walk the track as a way to unwind. I was just as stressed about the test as the men. This was the first group that had completed an entire unit with me, and walking not only helped me relax but gave me time to think without distractions. In class, we reviewed and talked, mostly about what was going on in the world, because I needed to keep them focused yet relaxed.

Maintaining Boundaries

Outside the Math 2 class, school enrollment was continuing to grow in general. One of the new students, Gangster, was so called because he pretty much fit the stereotype of your typical prison gangster. He was a tall, skinny black man with dreads. I don't know what he was "down" for, but he wasn't serving a life sentence. He had already been shot in the head twice and had spent over six months in the hospital.

He found his way to class early one day and asked if he could talk to me. We walked into the empty second classroom as men neared the school, and he pulled himself up to his full six feet seven inches and looked directly at me. "What you want? Why you care about us?" he said. "We gangsters. I been shot in the head twice, and when I get out, that will be my life—gangbanging." Tears filled his eyes. "No one can figure you out. What you doin' here? Nobody cares about us. Don't make no sense."

"I don't see any gangsters here," I told him. "Only students." And I walked away. As the men walked in, Gangster turned and wiped away his tears.

I always tried to encourage my students, but sometimes, they developed inappropriate attachments to me as a result. At the end of class that day, as I was sitting and working with another student, Gangster walked up, put his arm around me, and said, "This my wife. We getting married."

I didn't disrespect him in front of the others, but I stepped aside. At the end of class, I told him privately, "If you ever say that or touch me again, I will give you a report. I show you respect. You give it back."

He apologized, and I never had a problem with him again. Before he walked out that day, he turned around at Door Seven, shook his head, and whispered, "Thank you."

He transferred prisons, so I don't know if Gangster ever graduated. I hope he did.

MATH 2's FINAL EXAM

The day the rest of the Math 2 class was due to take their final exam, I watched the men as they walked over to the school. They weren't laughing or talking. Their heads were down, and they were moving very slowly. This only made me more nervous. I could tell they hadn't slept and still lacked confidence. I knew they could pass the test if they used the skills they learned, but I was concerned they would crash under pressure.

Jons was the first to leave the testing room. He came out smiling, with tears coming down his cheeks. He started pacing the floor. "Beth, I didn't just do this for my Mom," he said. "I did it for you. I can't believe I passed. I know it is against the rules, but I have to give you a hug."

He gave me a quick hug and sat down on the table with his head between his hands as we waited for more of his classmates to exit the testing room.

The next one out was Maro. He had a smile on his face, but he also looked disappointed. He looked at me and said, "Agent B, I knew I'd pass the test, but I thought I'd do better than I did." He passed with an eleven, which was still a good score.

Burt was next to exit the testing room. Like Jons, he had been reduced to tears, and he was shaking his head. "Beth, I can't believe it," he said. "I can't believe I passed." He was all smiles, and he shook my hand and thanked me. The three men who had finished hugged each other and sat beaming, waiting for Shorty to finish.

Shorty was the last to exit, and he came out with a seven, which was too low to pass.

"My reading wasn't good enough for the test," he said. "Why were there so many graphs?"

"You'll be fine when you take it again in two weeks." I tried to make it sound like no big deal. Somewhere down the line, students were going to fail, and it was good for all of them, including Shorty, to learn that now. The other men shook his hand and told him not to give up. They reminded him that because he had started the class late, he had had less practice than any of them. They didn't make fun of him, and they genuinely cared. Shorty took the time to congratulate the others even though I could see the sadness in his eyes.

Then they thanked me for helping them and headed, single file, down the sidewalk to their cells, with their heads held high and huge grins on their faces. Everyone in the pods knew they had achieved something.

When count was over and others came to school in the afternoon, they talked about it, congratulating those from Math 2 who were back in school that afternoon. There was excitement in the room for a long time after that. Even on the yard, as I would come to work, other offenders would tell me, "Teach, you did good!"

"No," I would respond. "These men did awesome, and I am proud of them."

Shorty came back to school that afternoon too. He had recovered from his morning's disappointment, and he came up to me with a smile.

"I'm all right," he told me. "I will pass because I know you will help me. You won't allow anyone to fail."

I reminded him that he had worked so hard that he had passed into the Math 2 class before anyone else in the previous course. He had been ready for the test, but it just hadn't been his day. I told him he needed to put in twenty hours of studying, test again, and then in two weeks, he would be sitting in that room again, hitting the submit button and passing the test. He said once again that I was crazy. I said I'd rather be crazy than boring. We studied while the other men worked on their writing class, and two weeks later, Shorty was sitting in the testing room, hitting the submit button, and crying himself. He had not only passed, he had earned the highest score in his class, a thirteen. He couldn't wait to call his family, his son. As he waited for the other men to leave school for the day, he looked back at me and said with a warm smile, "Thank you."

That afternoon, I walked the track after school, thinking about these men who had passed their math test and Robs's graduation. I had seen many students succeed over the years, but somehow, this meant more. I was watching men who had never believed their lives worth anything discover their minds had value. Almost every one of them had cried when he had seen that passing score; for the first time, he had achieved something important, and he knew it. My Math 2 students had not only learned the material, they had learned valuable lessons about life and hard work, and they were coming to realize their true potential. I was determined to spread those lessons to the entire prison school.

5

The New and Improved Prison School

*"Never believe that a few caring people can't change
the world. For, indeed, that's all who ever have."*
—Margaret Mead

Officers Dan and Roy, the tutors, and I had morphed into an amazing, inspirational, and cohesive educational team. My tutors, Shorty
and Shooter, along with the COs, brainstormed with me how we
could make the classroom in the newly built prison look more like
a school. We wanted this to be an active and vibrant classroom, so
my tutors used their creative minds to come up with a beautiful and
real-looking classroom, as compared to the old dark room we had
used before.

They worked hard at it, and when I was absent, Officer Dan monitored them so they could continue the changes, such as making copies,
designing bulletin boards, learning new material, typing, filing, and
otherwise improving the functionality and appearance of the room.
As the men walked into Door Seven, they looked around in awe at
the new classroom, filled with light and positivity, and the first display
they noticed consisted of two graduation hats, one on each side of the
whiteboard. Under one hat, a poster announced, "2016 Graduating
Class," and under the other, a second poster read, "2017 Graduating
Class." My tutors expected every student to fall into one of these two
categories. Those who had already graduated had their names typed
out, decorated with stars, and strung to the poster. I could hear the men

telling each other that their names would soon be up on the wall too. They pointed and smiled with excitement.

After the most recent graduation, graduates Flo and Redneck joined my roster of inmate-tutors, and the number of students attending school kept growing. Officer Dan was always there for me when I needed any help, as was Officer Roy. They kept a constant watch on the cameras to make sure everything was going smoothly. These two officers, along with many others, went above and beyond to help my students succeed.

We implemented a chart to keep track of student progress. This chart displayed each student's name marked with stars next to the tests they had passed thus far. This small yet profound addition to our classroom meant so much to the men because now they could readily see what they had accomplished. Soon, the new students saw their names and boasted they would be next to get stars. They became so excited that when it was their turn and they exited the testing room, they walked straight over to the poster to get their stars. The men smiled as they read all the posters and viewed the pictures of previous graduates on the walls. Shorty and Shooter had displayed pictures of former students working together, laughing, studying, and graduating.

In our new, active classroom, we had two huge maps—one of the world and one of the United States—hanging on the wall at the back of the room. We referred to them often while discussing history, and the men would point to places they had once lived or visited, reminiscing about their pasts, both the good and the bad.

Always present, however, was the need for safety. The huge white-board now hung to the back wall served a dual purpose. Puttied to this board were paper nametags of the students along with a schedule and roster for all classes and labs, which pleased Officer Dan because he could quickly see from the hall who was or should be in class.

There were six simple tables in our new classroom, with two chairs at each, and taped to the top of a table were the names of the students who would sit there. Students were partnered up with someone that they normally wouldn't hang out with in the yard. I learned quickly which men were part of which gangs and purposely seated them with members of other gangs or organizations. They weren't learning only subject areas but life lessons also. I still remember the look on Officer Dan's face when I showed him the seating arrangement. He looked at me and said, "Are you crazy?"

"It will be okay, Dan," I assured him.

He shook his head and muttered nervously as he walked out of the room.

If the men came to school for more than one class, they sat in the same seat, and this offered much-needed and appreciated structure. Change was tough on the men, even something as simple as a change of seats, so it was important to me that the school be a place they could come not only to learn but to get away from prison life. I wanted this to be a place where the men could put their guard down and just laugh, learn, and be part of something positive.

I had a beautiful wooden desk crafted by prison industries at the front of the room. I was not given a choice as to where the desk would be positioned, however, because the security warden wanted it placed so that I could get out of the room quickly if needed. The new prison had been constructed with strict security in mind. The wall along the entrance or hallway was constructed of windows so that as officers walked by, they could take a quick glance and unobtrusively check on people. The men saw officers continually walking by, which firmly established the fact that I was not alone, especially if Officer Dan was doing rounds.

The exterior wall, which looked out on the Native American sweat lodge, was where the tutors' computers desk was located. My tutors used their computers only for typing. Security would not allow them to have internet access. But even so, looking around, I felt that finally, this was the layout of an active classroom.

On the wall next to each exit door was a small whiteboard where I wrote announcements informing students of school closures and important testing dates. Inspirational posters hung on the walls. One favorite poster read "Eat, Sleep, Math." We had grammatical posters detailing the differences between "there," "they're," and "their," along with history posters and a poster of the periodic table. There was a sign on the door. It read, "Welcome to your new Educational Family. Thank you for taking the first step. —Beth."

I loved my huge whiteboard. I had been lucky enough to obtain a projector which allowed me to project all my lessons. I had taken equipment like this for granted in the high school where I had used to teach. We now had shelves filled with dictionaries and books on math, science, reading, Spanish, and history. We even had a few puzzle books and a section of magazines for light reading, including *National Geographic, Health Magazine*, and *People*. Of course, all our magazines, posters, and newspapers had been approved by the security warden before entering the Walls. Nothing could come in that wasn't first reviewed to ensure there was nothing inside that could compromise security.

I also now had a better way to communicate privately back and forth with my students. On top of the bookcase sat a huge wooden mailbox with thirty-two slots for the students' corrected assignments and lab work that they needed to complete.

We were ready to get down to work. The students came to school and were required to first take math, writing, and social studies classes. However, if they were at school and not in one of these classes, they would go to one of two new classrooms to work in study labs with tutors.

Some of these men hadn't used computers in years, so I encouraged them to work in the lab. I asked them to complete additional practice in their pods because there were a few computers available to them there outside regular class time.

Our lab was designed as a study room, where students worked on reading, typing, science, or homework from the other classes. If students were in a writing class, I required them to spend ten minutes a day in lab, typing in the classroom next to mine, and there was always an offender-tutor assigned to guide the men with their reading and typing in that room. The men would need to type an essay for the timed writing test, so it was important that they understood how and what to type and to do so as quickly as possible. Practice was imperative.

While the men typed, Tutor Redneck read with the men who struggled or were illiterate. I monitored the lab, entering every so often to answer questions and to make sure everyone was on task. Redneck had been tutoring at the school for only about six months before I left my position, but I knew he was a good fit because he showed sincere care, patience, and a desire to help these men. He worked with two men at a time, and all three of them took turns reading. I would listen as he complimented them on their progress, and every so often, I would go in and read with the men so that I too could acknowledge their advancements.

I held tutor meetings in the new school where I pointed out the great things they were accomplishing. I knew how crucial the inmate-tutors would be to the success of the prison school long after I had gone. The students learned from and respected their peers! But I had to be careful about what I allowed the tutors to do. At no point were the students to feel that the tutors were superior to them, and at no point were the tutors there to discipline or tell the students what to do. They were to work as guides, to help with assignments, and to be positive voices to keep the men motivated.

Shooter or Shorty worked in the two new classrooms and were usually available to guide the men if they needed help. I asked Shorty to be a tutor even before he graduated because of his incredible progress in math. During orientations, all the students were made aware of the tutors' duties, and they were assured that the tutors were not given answers for any of the assignments. We told them that the tutors were given the assignments ahead of time to review in their cells and would ask for help from me before class time. After that, the tutors and I would have some planning time where we could discuss their questions and concerns about how school was moving forward or, if it was not, what we needed to do to change that.

We held orientations approximately every three months, which coincided with the amount of time needed to complete a course. Orientations consisted of a PowerPoint presentation discussing all the school rules. We discussed testing procedures, minor and major reports, classroom behavior, accountability, teamwork, attendance, dress code, and what I saw as the most important part of the orientation: our "code." I acknowledged how proud I was of everyone who came through Door Seven for being brave enough to make a change. I also told them there would be days filled with laughter, hard work, successes, and failures. We would learn, fail, succeed, cry, and become one strong educational team together.

I was sure to share how I, too, had trouble with certain subjects, especially history. By talking about my background, which was in math, not history, I was able to show that we all have different strengths and weaknesses. I pointed out how we were to use our strengths to stand in for the weaknesses of others. By living that out in the classroom, I was hoping to teach them to model the constructive behavior of taking the high road when stepping up to help one another.

I addressed student language. Inside Door Seven, I explained, language was to improve. No one was to be teased or belittled when they struggled with the English language. I reminded them that I didn't care what brought them to prison or what gang they might be a part of or what their personal beliefs were. All I cared about was that they realized the opportunity they had every day that they entered Door Seven and made sure they were ready to move forward.

I explained the assigned seating in my classroom was nonnegotiable. If they didn't like who was at their table, they needed to get over it. In the real world, people work every day with people they don't care for. It's called rising above and being a productive member of a team. I was preparing them not just for testing but for life outside the walls. I can honestly say that I never had one issue with seating even though I purposely seated men next to each other who didn't associate together outside of class.

As class moved forward, the men started communicating more and more with their table partners. I would intentionally give them work that forced them to get to know their partner so they would begin talking to each other. Sometimes in writing class, I would have them write a paragraph about something they could both agree on was important in life. At other times, I gave them a math problem and asked them to solve it together at the board.

As students learned the routines and rules necessary to enter Door Seven each day, I noticed amazing things happening in school. The transition to managed enrollment meant that now, if students wanted to attend school, they would have to show up and complete their work. They could no longer merely show up to push worksheets around. We had stricter rules. After missing three classes without being excused, the student would be removed from the class enrollment. That student could apply to return during the next orientation, but even so, the penalty established the school's principle that the men needed to take school seriously or not attend. If a student did not complete a class in the allotted amount of time, he would have to start over with the next group of students. This upset the men, but it was a great teaching moment.

I told the students who had to repeat classes, "Now that you have gone through the class, even though you aren't ready for testing, you will be able to help other students in class. Remember how tough it was when you started? Others will struggle, too, so I'm happy I have you in this class again. Remember, we don't need to be in a hurry, especially when we are helping others." Just this little bit of encouragement went a long way toward establishing the kind of cooperative spirit I wanted to see in my classroom.

On the second day of the first managed enrollment class, students were asked to present their assignments. Three men had not completed their work, so I immediately called my officer to escort them out of my classroom and back to their units. None was under twenty-one, so no one was required to attend school.

"You are here to get educated," I told them. "You will graduate if you take school seriously, but if you are just here to get paid, this isn't the place for you."

The men were paid thirty cents an hour to attend school. For some, this was their only job, and that money could be an incentive for them. I stepped out in the hallway to have an extra word with these first three students, who were angry and disappointed to be thrown out. "Go back to your cells and think about what you want," I told them. "If you want a second chance, I would enjoy having you back in class. But perhaps now isn't the time for you to be in school. If that is the case, I will welcome you back in the future."

As Officer Dan walked them down the hall, I could hear the men complaining about me. "That bitch can't expect us to work! This is too hard," I could hear one say to another. "She is crazy to think we have time for this. It's fuckin' ridiculous."

I just winked at Dan and walked back through Door Seven.

Officer Dan was a big support for me, and so was Officer Roy, the camera guard up front. CO Roy always had a camera focused on the school and took great care of me. If I needed help with reports or rules or anything at all, he was a phone call or walk down the hall away. He often supported my rules, telling the men, "Do your work or don't come to school." It was as simple as that, and he often reiterated the need for the men to take school seriously and how, if they did so, tomorrow would be a better day.

The offenders would often complain to the guards and expect them to listen to their frustrations, but my COs didn't play along. In fact, Officer Roy would tell the men to quit whining. But he was respected by employees and offenders alike. His no nonsense attitude was kindly meant, and he didn't judge anyone. He just didn't allow the offenders to get away with things. He kept them accountable, and they knew not to cross the line with him.

The day after I dismissed my first three students, they returned to the school with cocky expressions and their heads held high. I could feel some tension, but I welcomed them back with a smile. The first two immediately showed me their completed work, but the third one had done nothing. I sent him back immediately with a stern warning: "That is strike number two. I want you in school, but I can't help you if you don't work."

He left with his head down. He didn't say a word. From that point on, I never had a problem with him or with any other student coming to class unprepared.

I didn't expect students to have all the correct answers. But I looked for an improvement in their work ethic as they continued with me in the prison school. My sternness with those three students early into the new program earned me respect. The other students knew I meant business. I had passed another test by being firm and consistent with the expectations I had established in orientation.

The next obstacle to conquer was tardiness. The men had a time span of ten minutes to get to class. That was five minutes before we started and up until five minutes after the beginning of class. We were a maximum-security prison; the men could not just come and go as they pleased. If they didn't show up for class, my officer was immediately on the phone or radio. And each day, students received passes for their next day at school. If a student who had received a pass exceeded the ten minutes he had to appear in school, he received a minor report for being out of their place of assignment.

The men tested me on this issue also, but I did not give in to them, and once they knew they wouldn't get away with being late, they were in class during their assigned times. The Department of Corrections was teaching these men not only about work ethic but about punctuality and accountability—important issues they probably never dealt with in the real world. They needed to learn reasoning skills, how to cope with different situations, how to think and act appropriately. Many offenders had never had a job in the free world, and so they didn't understand being on time, working with others, and being consistent. When they showed up on time for class, work in hand, they were learning about following a schedule, about respect, and the need to follow orders to maintain order.

As I mentioned before, in the beginning, the men's language was definitely unacceptable for school. In fact, it was basically unacceptable for civilization! So, to help them think more about their choices of words, I gave gentle reminders and subtle looks instead of calling them out in class. I recall one student telling me that he started doing twenty-five push-ups every time he swore outside of school. He said others were starting to do the same, and by the time I left them, these men carried themselves with more confidence. I no longer heard "homie, homes, fucker," and "I'm down with that, I feel you." The offenders spoke with less slang, putting more thought into the words they used. They stopped hiding behind their hair. Instead, they combed it. They brushed their teeth and stood proud, no longer slumped over! They had their chins up, smiling. They were becoming mature, confident men.

They were also truly becoming part of a team. I remember one student reading aloud in history class for the first time. I never thought he would do so because it was a struggle for him, and in prison, you don't show your weaknesses. Well, he did, and an amazing thing happened. As he was reading aloud that day and suddenly got stuck on a word, the person sitting next to him helped him pronounce it. I watched as men left class, shaking this man's hand, saying, "That was cool, man. You did great." This was a huge moment for all of us. That brave student who had had the strength to keep moving forward even with his poor reading ability, right there in class, opened the door for others to do the same. From that point on, I knew more amazing things would continue to happen behind Door Seven. The fences were coming down, and students like him were responsible for leading the way.

OFFICERS AND GENTLEMEN

Great changes were happening in the prison school. I had had the vision of what was possible back before the move, but it would have been impossible to execute without the input of my team—both my inmate-tutors and the incredible officers assigned to protect me.

I have mentioned Officer Dan before. I first met him about a month before we began the move to the new prison. He had been assigned to be my officer after the move. He was warm and welcoming from the start, and he became an integral part of my educational team, but our first day as partners was a bit of an adventure.

Shortly before this, there had been a fight among the offenders in the yard. This led to the implementation of a prison-wide lockdown until the move. As you might imagine, a monthlong lockdown occasionally causes even more problems. For example, one offender who had recently assaulted an officer was moved to the medical unit, where his cell would include a shower, in order to further limit his interaction with other inmates during the lockdown. Unfortunately, the isolation of the lockdown enabled him to find a way to escape. He shimmied up a pipe chase above his shower, which led to a vent to the rooftop. Supposedly, he put together over sixty feet of bed sheets that he used as a rope to aid in his escape from the prison roof. He was caught roughly one hundred miles from the prison.

The month up to our move to the new prison was extremely nerve-wracking for many of the men. Some had been housed in the old prison for more than twenty years. Many of them called it home. Now, they were moving to a new, unknown place. To add more stress, many of the men had their own cells for all these years and would now need to share a cell for the first time.

With the upcoming move and the lockdown on top of it, there was so much tension and unease in the prison that the powers that be had called for all hands on deck. All employees, including me, were not only put to work in places like the chow hall but also set to inventorying the men, to get them ready for their move so that when they were transported to the new prison, they would find their belongings already waiting for them in their new cell, as a way to ease the stress of the transition. The only things not to be boxed up were the things the prison inmates would carry with them on the buses the day of the move.

Officer Dan and I had a chance to get to know one another as we worked on the inventory together. One day, we were ordered to report to cell house 318. We began the inventory there, and Officer Dan realized the current offender we were working with, a man named Bill, would need another box to pack everything. He told me to keep checking off the man's belongings, and so I did as ordered while Officer Dan disappeared to find an empty box for Bill to use.

Suddenly, Officer Dan came running back in the room, almost in a panic. He looked at Bill and immediately asked if he was okay, wanting to make sure he was calm. The question seemed urgent. "Are you okay?" he asked again.

Bill didn't answer, so Officer Dan whipped around to face me. "Go stand outside the cell, Beth. Take a break while I finish the inventory," he said.

I had no idea what was going on, but I had been trained to follow orders, and something in Officer Dan's voice told me it was especially important this time. I walked out of the cell without saying a word.

When Officer Dan had completed the inventory of Bill's cell, he rejoined me. He explained how Bill, a small, skinny white man probably in his sixties, hated women and at no time should have been left alone with one. He had killed women in the past.

The news came as a bit of a shock to me. I had been completely unaware of the threat. "Wow, thank you for not allowing him to kill me," I said, chuckling shakily. "I could have probably taken him though." I was grateful Dan had remembered the danger, but I teased him for the rest of our time together for forgetting it, just for a moment.

It was another example of the constant need for awareness in a prison environment. Looking back, I probably could have benefitted from knowing about Offender Bill's crime, but for the most part, I stuck to my resolution not to ask about offenders' pasts so that I would be unable to judge. At the same time, I felt better knowing the officers in charge of my safety knew the details about all the offenders and would use them to keep me safe.

Officer Dan was quite the character. He sat in class with me while Unit One was in school, because once again, one of those men could not be left alone with a woman. I decided if he was to be in my class-room, I would put him to work. He read with three of the men who were illiterate each morning, and after the first day, I heard him telling the men that if they wanted to come to school, they needed to brush their damn teeth because they stank! I made sure to bring a few mints the next morning. Officer Dan kept me safe; I definitely wanted to keep him happy.

Another day, Officer Dan again sat in on class. Only a couple of students were in attendance, as well as Tutor Shorty, because the Unit Two men were on restricted movement and therefore couldn't attend class. I posed a question to the class. "What number squared is 25?" I asked.

Proudly, one student shouted out, "Five!"

"Yes," I replied. "Thank you. And what else?"

Puzzled looks crossed their faces, and all of them stared at the board, trying to figure it out. I smiled, shook my head, and went to the restroom, leaving them with Officer Dan to work out the answer.

When I walked out of the restroom, from the wall of windows, I could see that they were all sitting with Officer Dan, still trying to figure out the solution. So, I leaned up against the window and just watched for a bit. Someone said, "2.5," so Officer Dan asked Shorty to check that on the calculator. Nope. Someone said, "25," and Shorty declared that wouldn't work either. It was so awesome, as a teacher, to watch them trying to figure this out together. They must have worked on it for fifteen minutes, and I loved that they were talking and discussing, frustrated but not giving up.

I then walked back in the room, and they all looked expectantly at me.

"Are you are playing us?" Officer Dan asked. "There is nothing else times itself that is 25."

"Are you sure?" I asked. "How about -5?"

They looked at me, stunned, their mouths open, deep in thought. I could almost hear them thinking to themselves: *Does -5 x -5=25?* Finally, someone declared, "It is!" That is something I will never forget, and neither will any of them!

Officer Dan had worked in the prison for more than twenty years but was impressed by the work we were doing. He really enjoyed being part of the school. He and Officer Roy were always excited to hear if the men passed their tests. They shook the men's hands as they celebrated a passing grade and tried to cheer them up when times were tough.

A Second Major Offense

I could always count on my officers to have my back. Over the three years I taught at prison, occasionally the officers assigned to my classroom had to remove some of my students.

I could always count on Officer Roy, the cameraman for our school building and a vital member of our team, to be on the lookout for anything unusual. He was very supportive of the school, and his support was important to the men. He was always congratulating them for passing tests, encouraging them to keep working, and countering any negativity they tried to bring past the seventh door. But I knew I could rely upon him to keep me safe as well.

He watched the cameras from the front entrance and checked the men in the building as they entered the metal detector. When Offender Wheels wouldn't stop his staring, Officer Roy protected me and backed me up on my threat to have him removed from the school. Whenever I needed help with reports, he was there. If I needed to talk to an offender or needed to check to see if an offender was in the yard, he was on the cameras and ensured that the offender was brought to the school. Finally, if an offender was late for class, he and Officer Dan were on it.

Officer Dan would remove offenders from the school if he felt they would not change—those offenders with no concept of right and wrong who could indeed be a threat to society, posed any threat to me or to the other students, or were too worked up to be in school on any given day.

On one such occasion, a student made it quite obvious that he was staring at my backside every time I walked around the room. Many of the men stared at me, but this man created a scene, exaggerating his expression as I walked by him, worked at the board, or looked into the filing cabinet. It was his way of drawing attention to himself. In my eyes, at least, he was not ready to be in school. He needed to step away until he was truly there for the right reasons.

Another student, Bronx, had to be removed after a succession of decidedly wrong choices. Like others in my class, Bronx wanted my full attention, but he took it farther and often told Officer Dan that he was getting mad. He would complain to me, constantly reminding me that he had had a stroke and his memory was poor. He felt my time working with Unit One men should be given mainly to him. Obviously, that kind of one-on-one attention wasn't going to happen. I had eight students from Unit One who attended school, and they all needed help. As Bronx's frustration grew, Officer Dan, who had the training and experience to recognize the danger signs, decided to remove Bronx from class. Officer Dan approached me one day and informed me that he strongly felt Bronx was becoming a threat to me and that he should not attend school anymore. I offered to send classwork to Bronx's cell so his education could progress; however, Bronx declined.

A few weeks before leaving my position at the prison, I paid a visit to both current and former students, including Bronx. I wished him well and told him that a new teacher would be starting, and he might have better success with that person. He just looked through me and stayed silent.

Another time, when Officer Dan was standing outside in the hallway and Shorty was busy reviewing some math with the men, I noticed another man's pants hanging very low. I could see his underwear. He wasn't wearing a belt, which was against school rules. The warden required belts in school so none of the men would be able to pull their pants down easily. Sagging was prohibited.

I went out into the hallway to Officer Dan. "Look over at Mills," I told him. "His pants are hanging down."

Officer Dan shook his head. "Jeez, these men." He walked in the room and looked at Mills. "Pull your pants up," he ordered. "Where is your belt?" Mills replied that he'd lost it. Yeah, right.

"We'll continue this conversation after class," Officer Dan said.

As he walked away, Officer Dan looked over at another student, and I heard him exclaim, "What the fuck are you doing, Henner? Get your hands out of your pants. You aren't jacking off in school." Henner took his hands out of his pants and went on with class.

School progressed as usual. Nobody was surprised, and nobody laughed. As I entered the classroom again, I was relieved that Henner's interest had probably not been in me, as I had been outside of the room when the behavior began, and I was very thankful Officer Dan had been so alert!

But the very next day after he might have been written up for having had his hands down his pants, Henner came to class in a foul mood. "You'd better watch your back," he told me.

While the students had not been disturbed by his behavior the previous day, at this, they all broke out in whispers for him to shut up. They knew his threat was a *major* offense. I radioed for Officer Dan, who then had to walk him out. I never asked Henner why he made the threat, but for whatever reason, school was not his number-one priority that day. He wrote to me from the hole to apologize, saying he didn't mean to threaten me and would like to come back to school when he got out.

While I was not sorry for filing the report, I came to realize that Henner's reactive behavior was normal for some inmates. They didn't know how to act. If Henner had had the appropriate reasoning skills, he would have asked to be excused from school that day and stayed in his cell to deal with his issues. For many offenders, reactivity and inability to cope with stress and anger results in their sentence to prison in the first place. They need to learn better ways to cope.

After Henner served his time in the hole for threatening me, he did come back to school. He put out his hand to shake mine and apologized once again. All I was thinking was: *I really don't want to shake his hand.* But I did, of course, and headed quickly for the sanitizer afterward.

Aside from the pornography incident I related earlier, Henner's threat was the only other major offense I had to report during my time in the Walls. While there were other instances of more minor rule breaking, they were few and far between.

A Team Effort

Each day, a number of people came together to ensure the school day ran smoothly. Stan was the lumper (laborer) in our area. He was a hardworking man in his sixties, much older than most of my students. He took pride in his work, and he cleaned constantly, washing the bathrooms, floors, wiping windows, bookshelves, and making the rooms look immaculate. The floors just shined thanks to Stan.

Despite this, he and I had our differences. Stan struggled to understand why I didn't want him running the floor waxer—which made a loud, disturbing noise—while I was having class. Furthermore, one wall of my room was all windows, and he felt the need to wipe smudge marks while I was teaching. You can imagine this was a huge distraction to the men.

One day, Stan and I had it out. We both agreed to work harder to respect the other's work. I found times when he could wash the windows and clean the floors by going into another room or having him work on it during my prep time. I did my best to show him how much I appreciated his work. I added him to our team for the orientations and asked him to say a few words about his work and how he was a crucial member of our team. In his turn, Stan requested that the men be respectful and keep our classroom clean. He wanted them to have a nice place to come to. We took to calling him our custodial engineer, and he worked hard to earn that title.

My Tutors

I appreciated everyone who helped me in the school, but I was always most grateful to my inmate tutors, Shooter and Shorty. It was their patience and work with their student peers that allowed the prison school to truly begin to thrive and grow.

Shooter was always respectful and appreciative in the classroom, a calm and patient presence that encouraged everyone who worked with him. He treated the men with such respect, never looking down on any of them for their weaknesses. He looked past any arrogance, and even when the men would get angry, he had a way of calming them down without ever raising his voice.

Shooter had been given a life sentence at the age of sixteen for kidnapping and sexually assaulting a sixteen-year-old pregnant girl. I know this only because an officer brought it to my attention one day before I could explain that I didn't want to know about his crime.

Officer Dan and Officer Roy, however, had already shared how they had seen a real change in Shooter over his years in prison. They said he'd grown up and really cared about people now. Over the time we worked together, Shooter never spoke of his crime, yet I could sense he felt remorse. I could see the sadness in his eyes, even though he was always positive at school. He was very protective of me and never wanted to see any women injured. He told me once that if anyone tried to hurt a woman, he would be the first to step in. I didn't respond. He was still an offender. But I believed in his sincerity. He proved time and again that he wouldn't put up with any disrespect toward officers or staff.

Shooter is now thirty-four years old. As one of the offenders affected by the new laws regarding juveniles who were handed down life sentences, he now has the chance for parole. He can go in front of the parole board each year, asking for a second chance. His last hearing went very well, probably because his resume now details years of hard work and positive contributions to the well-being of others in the Walls. He recently found out that he is being granted parole. ICE will pick him up soon, and he will be sent back to his birthplace. The parole board is recognizing that he is now a new man who has grown up and changed.

Prison life has been harder on Shooter because of the nature of his crime. I heard through the grapevine that in prison, if you've hurt a child, you don't walk the yard for free. Offenders will not tolerate men who have hurt children. Child molesters or inmates who have hurt a child in any manner are not accepted by the other offenders. The only way to stay safe is to pay for protection or go to into protective custody, or PC. Protective custody is like being in the hole. Men can be placed in PC without asking, because it is also the DOC's job to protect the offenders. If security feels an inmate is in danger, that inmate will be sent to PC or be transferred to another facility.

Despite or because of his past difficulties, I truly believe Shooter is evidence that people can change. Not to say that Shooter is perfect. At one point, I heard he was up to no good in the computer lab, running a business downloading pornography onto flash drives for the men. I did not confront him on this, because I could never officially verify it, so I took a different tack, and I closed down the lab. I saw a sudden change in Shooter. I wondered if he was scared that he couldn't complete his work. If he gave someone his word that he would download something onto a drive for him and didn't follow through, that would hurt his reputation. Your word is everything in prison. But then I wondered, had I heard wrong? Was he truly downloading pornography? Was he perhaps upset with me for not confronting him? Maybe he truly wasn't doing anything wrong. There are many jealous people in prison, and sometimes the men don't like to see others succeed. Shooter had a lot going for him. He worked as a tutor in the school, which was a job only a few out of over seven hundred could have. He was educated, and now he had the opportunity that many dreamed of: possible parole. Whether Shooter had been guilty of running a pornography business or not, for a while after I shut down the lab, his performance in school suffered. My respect for him did not. I appreciated all the amazing ideas he brought. He cared about the program, and he wanted the men to succeed. He loved teaching.

I still speak with Shooter today, and he is doing amazing things in prison. He continues to tutor men, helping with the Anti-Violence Program and working as a translator. He has taken college courses and continued to score well, and now he has earned his paralegal's certification. He has a love for learning and is thankful for every breath he takes. When he walks out of those steel doors, it will be as a man very different than the one that walked in, with much to offer the world. Shooter has a lot of good qualities that he is developing every day and every year in prison. I learned so much just by observing him. He is also an outstanding writer and is currently writing a book about his life. Someday, when he leaves prison, his plan is to publish it. I look forward to reading it one day.

Shooter changed in the years before I began prison work, but over the time I worked in the Walls, I saw an equally dramatic transformation in Shorty, my other inmate tutor. Originally from Mexico, Shorty is serving a life sentence without parole for felony murder. Unfortunately, the laws in the state in which he committed his crime mandate that if a felony is committed and someone dies as a result, anyone involved receives a life sentence regardless of which person involved caused the death. So even though Shorty was not the shooter the day he was involved in the felony, was in fact unarmed, and ran when the gun was fired, he was equally liable for the offense. He was eighteen years old and had never been in trouble with the law before. He has been in prison for twenty years now. His mistake resulted in a lifelong incarceration.

Not that he was an innocent inside the Walls. As I mentioned before, I had heard when Shorty began attending the school that he was possibly a gang leader within the prison. When I decided he should be a tutor because of his high score in the new testing program, his work ethic, and his kindness toward the other students, I insisted that if he truly was the head of his gang, he had to step down. "I don't want any gangbanging in school," I told him. Without hesitation, he agreed. He wanted to be a tutor. He did not admit to having been a gang leader or a member of any gang, and throughout our work together in the school, I never saw any signs of gang behavior from him. But shortly after he became a tutor, an officer at the prison took me aside.

He looked at me for a moment. "Who are you?" he asked.

"What do you mean?" I replied.

He said, "Shorty stepped down from the gang for you. That just doesn't happen. He has been the leader since he came in twenty years ago. You normally can't just step down, but the gang has allowed him to do so. That is unbelievable. You have truly changed this man."

The officer told me that in more than twenty years of working at the prison, he had never seen anything like this happen. I just smiled.

It would not be the last time I would hear something similar over the course of my three years teaching in the Walls. I always explained that I was not with the men in their cells. Whatever they decided to do away from the school represented their own personal choices to learn, to improve—whether, to them, that meant having better, more interesting communication with family members; receiving a diploma to show their parents and kids that they were improving; or simply showing up others in prison. Whatever their reasoning, they chose to walk through Door Seven and to make all the choices elsewhere to do well there.

School meant a lot to Shorty. He was the person who initiated a rule that students should do twenty-five push-ups for each swear word they spoke. The other students followed his lead. Eventually, Shorty's own swearing disappeared, and words like "homes" and "homie" were no longer part of his vocabulary.

Shorty came to work every day, never missing one. I worked with him on math every chance I had, because he always wanted to learn more. He would go up to the board and work problems for the men, and he also helped with math labs. The men appreciated it, and he said he felt so amazing; never in his life had he thought he would be teaching men algebra. His eyes sparkled when he was teaching, and he always had a huge smile on his face. He told me that I made him smart, and it was the best feeling in the world. Privately, he told me that there was something about me, and how with me as the teacher in their school, all the men wanted to be there. They appreciated that I truly cared and they could see it. This is why I was there!

At school, Shorty's help made me feel safer. I knew he would not allow anyone to hurt me. He didn't say it; I just knew it. There were no fights in the three years I worked in the school, and I am sure he had something to do with that. Every other place in the prison, there were fights—in the yard, chow hall, chapel, card room, library, and the units, but not in our school. The classroom became known as the "safe zone."

It became a place where the men felt they were away from prison life for a while. They felt like they were free.

Shorty was always watchful and paid close attention to the students and their intentions. When new men came into the prison, some, who had already heard of him, wanted to meet him, and they tried to come down the hallway to meet him. But Shorty would tell them that unless they were attending school, they couldn't come in without a pass. I could never thank Shorty. That would be to turn his actions into a favor to me, which was against the prison rules. But, at the same time, I appreciated Shorty and the other tutors' maintaining order around our school. For some reason, everyone wanted to enter the Seventh Door, even if it was just to poke their heads in to say hi. But my tutors would stop them and inform them of the school rule.

Every morning at 7:05, I would hear Shorty singing as he came to work. He was so happy to be there. Officers told me that he encouraged and assisted the men in his unit outside of school. He would tell students to make sure they got a good night's sleep before testing, and he even went as far as to walk out on the basketball court during a game to remind students who had tests in the morning.

Everyone remarked on how much he had changed. As we got to know one another better, I learned that Shorty was beaten as a young boy by his father and never had support at home. He talked about all the scars he carried on his back from those early beatings. He needed someone to believe in him. I was that someone, and his pride in his work at school helped turn him around. Now, his family was proud of him as well. At graduation, Enrique, Shorty's son, said that his dad was now not only well spoken but happier as well. Every time he spoke with his dad, he could hear positive changes. Enrique thanked me and shared how Shorty had so much more to offer during their phone conversations now that he was speaking better English, reading, listening to the news, and getting educated.

Unfortunately, not everyone in the Walls was receptive to the positive changes they saw in Shorty. Shorty told me that, quite often, the officers came to his cell with chains to bring him to lockup. He said that, even when he had done nothing wrong, sometimes he would be taken to the hole. At first, I doubted Shorty's allegations, but a certain incident in the prison made me start believing him.

One morning, Officer Dan and I walked in behind Officer Roy. Officer Roy turned around and shouted down to us, "Shorty is in lockup. He wants you both to know he did nothing wrong and he'll be out soon."

As I walked in, I noticed there was no activity in the Walls, so I knew we were on restricted movement. Usually, offenders were walking to work or the chow hall at this time of the morning, and there would be officers and K9s outside watching. That morning it was quiet. When I entered the building, I went down the hall to my classroom. Officer Dan had to wait behind to punch in for work. When he entered my classroom, he told me there had been a fight the night before in the chow hall and that we were on lockdown. "It could last for some time," he told me, "because it may be gang related."

"What happened?" I asked.

"Offender Slash was stabbed in the side of his jaw, by his ear, and it was pretty bad."

"Could I watch it on camera?"

I wanted to see for myself what happened. The camera showed a man coming up behind Slash, who was sitting at his small, round table with Shorty and Vegas, another one of my students. The man stabbed Slash, and blood squirted everywhere with every pulse of his heart. Red stains spread on the table and chairs. Slash jerked up to fight his attacker. The two men rolled on the floor, throwing punches to each other's faces. Slash ended up on top of the man who stabbed him and was punching him with all he had. Officers were there and moved to separate them, but when they were separated, Slash was still on the ground, and an officer was holding his hand against the side of his face, trying to stop the blood flowing from the wound.

Thanks to the officer's fast reaction, Slash survived the stabbing. But as I watched and rewatched the video, I couldn't help thinking that something looked off. I focused on the other offenders, not on the fight. Shorty and Vegas, who had been sitting at the table with Slash, never even flinched when he was attacked. They just kept eating as if nothing happened. One time, I saw Shorty look over to Vegas and say something, and they both looked down at the men fighting on the floor.

The prison rule does state that offenders are to sit or get down on a knee if there is a fight, and so these two followed the rules by continuing to sit. In fact, everyone continued to sit. I can honestly say that I would not be able to continue eating, especially with all the blood splashed over the table, but these men did. In still another viewing of the recorded video, I noticed that, before the attack, the man who stabbed Slash walked by the table where Shorty was sitting. He nodded, and a man from a table behind Shorty responded with a sign and a good job. The attacker then continued out with the officers.

Security thought Shorty had ordered the hit on Slash because he hadn't flinched during the fight and, more importantly, because he had spoken to the attacker ahead of time. When I investigated the incident, I learned that the actual conversation had nothing to do with the attack. Shorty was asking the man whether a student had been in for supper yet because he wanted to talk to him about the test he was taking the next morning. His story checked out from what I knew of Shorty and his current behavior in the prison. I believed he and Vegas hadn't flinched during the attack because of all the violence they had witnessed in their lives. Perhaps they were stunned. Perhaps this attack just didn't faze them.

Shorty was in lockup, waiting for the investigation to end. All eyes had been on him, but Officer Roy, Officer Dan, and Officer Renee did not believe he had ordered the hit on Slash. They had seen the positive changes in Shorty, and they wanted to believe in him, knowing that he had always helped and shown respect to Slash in class. I also knew Shorty wasn't guilty. He was too proud of his progress in school to mess it up with something like this. He loved being in school; it gave him a reason to wake up every morning. He had told me that before he had worked at the school, he had used to pray to God to die in his sleep because he had nothing to live for. But now he had something.

But I heard security wanted Shorty to be guilty of ordering the hit. He was doing so well in school that they wanted him out. They wanted him to go to the hole. Prison had its own rules, and gossip ran rampant inside the prison walls. Someone even went as far as to mention that he wouldn't be surprised if some kind of contraband was thrown into Shorty's cell, just so security could send him to lockup. I think he was joking, but that ticked me off. So, along with Officer Renee, I went to the deputy warden and the investigating officer. We explained what we had seen in the video.

We told them we didn't believe Shorty was guilty. He hadn't been acting any differently that day. Graduation was coming up, and his family was flying from miles away to attend, so if he got locked up, he wouldn't be able to attend the ceremony and see his family. Also, a production company was filming a documentary on Shorty, and the producers planned to film his graduation. He had too much to lose, and I knew in my heart and in my head that he wasn't guilty. My two officers, Dan and Roy, who always had my back, also called the investigator and said they didn't believe he was involved in the stabbing.

Shorty did finally get out of lockup, but it took at least two weeks. And because I had defended an offender, my situation changed. I was later told by second-shift officers that they were to watch me closely whenever I was with Shorty. They had officers Dan and Roy watching me nonstop, even when both had stuck up for me and asserted I treated all my students with the same support and respect. To their credit, my officers did not tell me how they were watching me, but I sensed it. I didn't hold a grudge against the officers for doing their jobs, but I had to watch my behavior more closely to make sure I exhibited no favoritism.

I was no longer allowed to eat lunch with Shorty, even though we were on camera the entire time. In one month's time, he and Shooter, who were roommates as well as fellow tutors, were shaken down eight times. I wondered if security suspected me of bringing in contraband for them. The very idea was laughable. The shakedowns were a waste of everyone's time. Security never found anything.

I spoke to administration about the increased pressure on me and on my tutors. She replied, "You're only at school to teach the men, not talk to them."

I could not believe that she had said that. "These are my students," I told her. "I am not security. I will treat them with respect, and I will talk to them. If I am doing something wrong, please tell me, but know that I will walk out of here with my head held high."

I was being bullied, and that was as unacceptable as any other behavior that needed correction in the prison. Shorty had done nothing wrong, and I was not going to stand by while he was wrongly accused, so I had done what I felt was right. There was a double standard in the prison. The security people had no trouble going to Shorty when they wanted his help. According to another inmate, security would go to Shorty when they needed someone to talk to the men to settle things down. They used him, but they wanted to ensure he always remained under their control.

Shorty once told me that he felt he was an alien on this planet. At the new prison, he could get a glimpse of cars driving by, and he would wonder where they were going. When tours came in, he said, he felt like an animal in a zoo. He knew they were coming to look at the criminals; they didn't care about the facility. He said the only time he felt the same as everyone else was when he looked at the stars. His eyes misted as he said, "We all see the same stars, and none of us will ever reach them." His perfect words clearly described our human commonality.

Shorty couldn't understand why he had to die in prison. He had never killed anyone. He felt awful for what had happened, but, he asked, wasn't twenty years enough time served? When he was sentenced to die in prison, he had not even understood. He was not yet that proficient in English. Can you imagine never even having a speeding ticket, coming to the United States from Mexico for a better life, just to die in prison? Shorty's story is one of the reasons I am so passionate about prison reform.

Today, Shorty has transferred to another prison and, like Shooter, continues to tutor students in math. He fights every day for his freedom—reading, researching, writing letters, hoping someone will hear his story and help him. He committed his crime when he was eighteen. As I write this book, he has been in prison for more than twenty years. When is enough enough? There are many people in the prison system who actually have taken a life yet serve less time or have a chance at parole. Shorty does not have this chance, even though the crime he was sentenced for was his first offense. He wants one chance to show everyone that he can be a positive asset in the free world, and although he has a life sentence without parole, he will not give up. He is helping and will continue to help others, leading by example. He works hospice and encourages the men to write final letters. His goal is to help inmates learn to respect others.

Shorty and I still speak as well. He tells me how he has learned the value of life and not to take it for granted. He is working to instill this thought in all the men. He is especially inspired to make a difference in the lives of young men, knowing that perhaps they will receive a second chance. He wants to help prepare them by teaching them about respect, accountability, cleanliness, and the importance of an education. One time, he told me a story of how he was helping a student who hadn't spoken to his father in years. The man didn't want to reach out because he knew his father was ashamed of him, but he listened to Shorty and finally wrote a letter to his father, telling him how sorry he was and that he loved him. The man cried when his father responded positively. That inmate will be getting out of prison someday and hopefully now he will have a relationship with his father. Shorty is paying forward the difference that education made in his life, making a difference in the lives of others.

In the Lockup

Both Shorty and Shooter were always grateful for the clothes on their backs and the food they had to eat. It is one of my strongest memories of them. They remember the days outside the Walls where they went hungry because they had nothing to eat. So they were appreciative for the very basics of life, even when they found themselves in the hole.

Their attitudes inspired me. Both Shorty and Shooter spent time in the hole, and so did many of my other students, for one reason or another. Eventually, I decided that there was no way I was going to allow the men who had successfully walked through Door Seven but somehow managed to find their way back into lockup to neglect their educations in lockup. *School must go on*, I thought. I sent them mail with homework through the prison mail system.

If I didn't receive work back in a reasonable amount of time, I paid my students a visit. As soon as I walked into the pod, all the inmates knew I was there.

"The teacher is here," someone started yelling. "She has jeans on. I've never seen her in jeans before."

104

They talked as though I was not there. I tried not to worry about it too much. Even on days I did wear jeans, I always wore a top that was long enough to cover my behind. The men were going to make comments. I had learned quickly that I had to have thick skin. The way I looked at it, I was well liked, and that made me lucky. None of the men threw semen, stools, or spit at me. None of them attacked me as they had others in the past. So, what they said—even though it wasn't conversation I would share with my family at dinner—didn't bother me. I always walked with confidence. I could write reports about their foul mouths, but once I started, I would be writing reports nonstop.

Once, as I walked past a cell, a man said to the offender in the cell next to him, "Did you see that ass when she bent over? This bitch is thick, just the way I like them."

I looked him in the eyes and asked, "Are you saying I'm fat? What does *thick* mean?"

"Solid, like you work out," he said.

"Good cover. Don't say it again, or I will write you a minor." I made light of the situation, showing confidence and lack of interest, an attitude that helped me every time I had to go to lockup.

As I visited pods, others hollered, "Cell 23, cell 19, stop by please."

Usually, I didn't stop during my visits to lockup. I learned that if I stopped by every cell, I would be there all day.

But one day, someone shouted, "I have a memo for you, Teacher. Would you stop by on your way down?"

"Sure," I called back. I stopped at the cell and asked, "You have a memo?" And as I looked in the little rectangular window in the cell door, I could see inmate Freckles, standing nude and masturbating in front of me.

"Please come in, please come in," he said.

I just walked down the stairs to the officer's desk and reported his actions to the officer.

"Freckles does this to everyone," the officer said. "It's up to you if you want to write him up."

I looked down the row and saw Inmate Freckles still staring out his window, looking at me. *He needs help*, I thought. He was so messed up in the head. I remembered seeing him in the yard. He had always been polite out there. Eventually, I heard he killed his girlfriend and then had sex with her. I shook my head and went back to the school. I could help some, but I couldn't help them all.

I told Officer Dan about this incident. Of course, he found some way to make me laugh over it. The next time I needed to go to lockup, he said, "I want to go with you."

I took him up on the offer, and the next time I walked into a pod, when the men began yelling, Officer Dan yelled back. "The teacher is here," he called. "Does anyone have a memo for her? Memos, anyone?"

I just shook my head and quietly laughed. Sometimes, you just have to go with it.

Another time, one of the men asked if I would critique a letter he had written for a writing contest. The contest was over, but he wanted to know what I thought. The teacher in me spoke first, and I said I would do it and get back to him. I did not look at the letter until a couple days later. Only then did I realize the letter was all about me and how he liked smart women. He was turned on by thinking of having an intelligent conversation with me. He wanted to marry me and thought we were a good match because we would have brilliant kids. He mentioned he wanted to take me out on a date. I wondered if he thought he could escort me down to the chow hall. He had a life sentence, so where else could we go? The letter this particular inmate wrote to me got him a longer stay in Unit One, and thereafter, he was not allowed to enter the school hallway without a reason and an escort.

The prison system all too often acts as cages for people, treating them as animals rather than seeking to reform them as it ought. As strange as this may sound, many of the men in lockup just wanted to smell me, not necessarily to talk to me. As I passed through the lockup, they would call, "I can smell a woman in here." Later, I found out that some of the men had such a strong sense of smell that they could tell when a woman was menstruating.

At times, with all the noise in the pods, I never could tell who was saying what. I learned to get in and out quickly. I talked to those I needed to but respectfully declined most others. I would always stop at a few cells out of deference but then say I had to get back to school. Rudeness was usually more annoying than frightening. Besides, I had work to do, and eventually, I was the only teacher in the school. The objectionable chatter I heard in lockup stemmed from boredom and immaturity. I was strong, and it wasn't going to break me. I could walk away from it.

It also always came from inmates who didn't attend the school. My students were always respectful, and they were the reason I made my excursions to lockup.

When I showed up unexpectedly, I could see the smiles on my students' faces. They respected me for taking the time to check on them, and they appreciated my willingness to do so despite what I went through to get to them. I believed in them, something most of them had never experienced before. Visiting lockup was a big deal for both the men and for me. It showed all the men in the prison that I wasn't scared and I was doing my job the way it needed to be done. Even more men started to attend school. They knew I was not going to give up on them. I was tough and followed through. They also knew that, if they got sent to lockup, their educations would not go on lockdown, at least not in my eyes.

I established a routine with all my students. If the prison went on lockdown, I went through the units to give and collect classwork. When they saw me coming, the pods got noisy, and the students all smiled. I wasn't letting them down, and I wasn't going away when times got tough. They would stop sleeping or watching television and focus on their educations. They knew they had things to do and important things to accomplish.

Because many inmates already had their diplomas, they weren't allowed at school unless they were illiterate. Unfortunately, there were men with diplomas who tested as illiterate. Sometimes that was because they had tested when they first came to prison and didn't have the mindset to care about a test. If they came to school for reading, I first tested them again to make sure they qualified and were in fact illiterate. If they were not, I would still accept memos from them and look things up if they were appropriate. One man wanted math that dealt with carpentry work, while another person wanted to learn about Abraham Lincoln.

As an educator, I was happy to send educational materials out for any of the seven hundred inmates to read and learn. I would carry a notebook when I visited the units. As the men asked for different materials to read, I would have them send a memo to me. Once I received the memo, I could then send them what I had already prepared. I felt education didn't have to stop at the exit of the Seventh Door, and helping men outside of the school learn was another opportunity to earn respect from the inmates.

When men in lockup were close to graduating, I would cancel my lab time and go to lockup for them. The pods had classrooms, and the men could be shackled and brought there. They would be cuffed by their feet and one wrist to a bar on a desk, but they would have one hand free to write, and they could continue and complete their classes. They didn't have to forget what they had learned.

I realized in my work in the units, and especially in lockup, that I looked at men in the hole differently than people in the security department. Many men struggled with the security officers.

An offender once told me, "You can tell the difference between criminals and those of us who are here because of a poor decision. True criminals had many beefs with law enforcement before coming to prison, and it shows when they speak to officers with no respect. Those of us who have no past offences don't take everything out on the officers. We don't blame them for our being here, and we don't show hatred toward them."

I remember one officer once told Offender Cilo, "Don't give the teacher a hard time."

"We like Beth," Cilo responded. "She is safe with us. No one will hurt her."

6

Education for All

Nobody cares how much you know,
until they know how much you care.
—Theodore Roosevelt

Inside the prison school, we began innovating ways for the men to prepare for their tests. We held math competitions in class to help the men prepare for the HSED math test. For a change of pace, I would put multiple-choice problems up on the board, and they would raise their fingers—1, 2, 3, or 4, depending on which answer they felt was correct. They loved doing this, and I would sit in the back of the class, tallying their answers and using a wireless mouse to switch the problems projected on the board.

They would raise their hands high in the air, covering up their fingers so only I could see their answers. Sometimes, we would quickly try to get in one more problem before they had to leave class because they were having so much fun, and the competition was usually close. My students Lupin, Bronx, Coles, and May competed often when they were in the same math class. Lupin would jump up and down with excitement, and Bronx would come in each day asking, "Can we compete again?" I made sure that the we spent the last two weeks before testing doing just that.

Lupin called me "Teacher Lady." He shared that his girl was pregnant, and he wanted to change his life for his son. He had a gang tattoo on his face that he chose to have burned off as proof of his desire to better himself. Although Lupin struggled in school, he worked so very hard.

He took the science test first, coming to school and studying in the lab a few hours each day when he wasn't in math class. Unfortunately, he did not pass the practice test on his first try, and he was really mad at himself, so mad that he wanted to quit school. Shooter and Shorty explained how difficult testing is and said that he would get through it.

"Lupin, it is your first test," I told him. "You missed it by only one point! We will practice test again in a couple weeks, and I'm sure you'll get it. Be patient. Your work ethic will pay off. Don't you give up on me."

The other men, as well as the tutors, told him to keep working, but that first failure was tough on him. I told him what I told all the students after a test: "Go back to your cell and relax. We will get back to work tomorrow."

The next morning, Officer Dan stopped by my room and asked me to take a walk with him. We walked to the end of the hallway, and he opened the door to the cardroom. At first glance, it looked empty, but when I stepped inside, there was Lupin. He had all his books out, and he was studying. "Hi, Teacher Lady," he said.

"Lupin," I told him, "you just made my day. Do you need help with anything?"

He said he was fine, that he was just looking for a quiet place to study, and Officer Roy told him he could be in there.

We left the room, and once we were out of earshot, Officer Dan told me, "I never saw anything like this in all my twenty years. They didn't study before you came here. They didn't give a shit about anything." We headed back down the hall to the classroom, and again he muttered, "I just have never seen this before."

In another two weeks, it was time for Lupin to test again. He had already passed the practice test in science and was ready for the real test. He looked very tired. I was concerned. I knew I had to distract him. I asked him how his new son was getting along because he was always so excited to talk about him. He shared that his son had rolled over, and he proudly pulled out a picture from his pocket. Then he was called over to test. I continued with writing class while Lupin tested.

Suddenly I heard him yell from the testing room, "I passed!" He came over to the classroom with tears of joy in his eyes. "I passed, Teacher Lady, I passed!"

I smiled and let out a sigh of relief. He needed to pass that second test, or I knew he might've given up. This was his first success, but now I was confident he would continue, no matter how tough things got.

He said, "I have to go call my baby's mom and tell her." The other men in the room smiled, shook his hand, and some gave him a side hug.

Moments like these were the times I felt I was making a difference as a prison teacher. Not just because men were passing tests but because they were experiencing success, many for the first time in their lives. They were proud, they recognized their potential, and they were making a positive change in their lives. It was pretty awesome to see.

MATH WITH A SIDE OF ENGLISH, PLEASE

Math was not the only subject that I had to teach the men. The first writing class I taught was challenging for all of us. I soon learned that writing and math were the toughest tests for the men to pass.

In writing, we went through and learned all the grammar rules. I gave sentences filled with errors to the men so that they could make corrections with their table partner. They would then pass their corrections to the team behind them, who would make any corrections they felt were still necessary. We kept doing this until the papers made it back to the first students who worked on them. Then, each team would make the corrections on the whiteboard, one at a time, working from their papers. Because the work they wrote on the whiteboard came from the entire class, the men weren't scared of making mistakes in front of others. They were encouraged to go to the whiteboard more often. We discussed each sentence correction in class, and in writing and in the other classes I taught, I saw the men begin to contribute more. They eventually began volunteering to go to the whiteboard on their own.

Good Changes

I had found another key to motivate the men, beyond the thrill of competition. The men were having fun learning in school, and it was so wonderful to witness that. They were laughing and working well with their partners, and the entire class was coming together, a class of every color, creed, and background. Men were studying outside of class, and counselors and officers told me they were helping offenders with their class assignments.

Everyone was coming together to make change happen. Officers began to speak to me in passing: "I hear some men are testing today. Hope they pass." Staff was taking an interest in the school, something I had never noticed at the old prison. I don't know if it was because more men were graduating or because the school was more visible to everyone, but something special was going on.

Conversations in the Classroom

Because the prison classroom was a safe zone, the men began speaking of things other than the study material when they came through Door Seven. They liked to talk about the future. Many of the men often talked about going home and becoming rich with music, writing, or art. Although some were very talented in these areas, I wanted them to have more realistic expectations and to understand life was more than money and material things. So, when I found an opportunity to discuss life with them, I took it.

One year, when Valentine's Day was coming up, one of the men was talking about buying flowers for his girl, lamenting that he didn't have any money.

"Why do you need money?" I asked him.

"How do you buy flowers without money?" he asked.

I suggested we talk a little about life and women. "First, you don't need to buy your girl flowers because it is Valentine's Day," I said. "That is not a reason to buy flowers. Second, I have seen the talent many of you have. So instead of buying flowers, why don't you draw her flowers or write her a song? That would mean so much more than something bought at a store."

I tried to explain to my students that happiness doesn't come from money. Happiness comes from within. Only you can make yourself happy. No one else can do that. We had many talks about how to be happy without money and how dating doesn't need to always involve it.

I shared how spending time with your kids doesn't need to cost anything either. The men always listened to what I had to say, and I was grateful, but I didn't know if they believed me. I decided to attempt that subject from a different perspective. It was time to let them know that I knew what it felt like to be poor.

I shared with them how my father was a miner and my mother a homemaker. Creativity was often my entertainment. I have made a habit of frugality throughout my life. I wanted to share that habit with my students, so that they wouldn't leave prison with unattainable expectations. I felt compelled to teach them about careful spending, so they wouldn't fall back into hustling in order to maintain a lifestyle that really isn't essential for happiness.

We talked about the value of money and differing costs of living across the nation. My students often asked me questions about the cost of clothes, cars, food, and electronics. For the inmates who had been in for the last fifteen or twenty years, I could see that the numbers I quoted worried them.

Sometimes, I wasn't able to help them in understanding the prices of goods. I don't buy new cars or expensive electronics, so I couldn't tell them about the cost of those items. They weren't important to me, but they were important to my students.

Many of my students were surprised to learn that my clothes were off-brand. They commented that I dressed "rich." I said no, I was just "cleaned and ironed." They found this amusing. It was good to know that they were really listening.

REDNECK

Many of my students and tutors had colorful personalities despite or because of their difficult pasts. Redneck was one of those interesting people. He gave himself his nickname. I can remember his first day of school, when he walked in the door, and I extended my hand and said, "Hello, you must be Mr. James."

He looked at me and said, "I look like a redneck, and I talk like a redneck. We will get along just fine if you call me Redneck."

A white man in his fifties, Redneck had long blond hair, missing teeth, and some slang talking going on. He walked with a crutch because he needed his ankle replaced. He had attended school for more than ten years before I became the teacher. He hadn't yet passed one class, and therefore, he had never graduated and could keep coming to school year after year. I could tell he came just to check it out and he had no plans of graduating.

When I spoke with him about it, he told me he was dumb but that he would begin trying. The first test he passed was in social studies. He worked hard and studied all the time. After completing the test, he sat and just cried for a long time. He had never before passed anything in his life.

Redneck's first success inspired him. He set out to conquer math next. One day he came to class looking exhausted. I asked him if there had been a party in the unit because he looked hungover.

"No," he said. "I studied math until 2:30 in the morning, and then I had a bad dream about you. I woke up in sweats because all I could hear was you telling me, 'Eat, Sleep, Math! If you want to graduate, you need to work for it.'"

He went on to say that his shirt had been soaked. He hadn't been able to go back to sleep, so he started studying again. He was now ready to learn every day. He told me that he had wanted to graduate before his mom passed away because he had promised her he would. His mom had passed away the year before I came to the prison, but Redneck still wanted to keep his promise.

After Redneck passed his first test, a few more inmates signed up for school. Redneck had told everyone of his success, and the men couldn't believe it. A couple of months later, Redneck was ready to test in math. He passed again.

The next day, he walked into class with his head held high and said, "I am a student." He now knew he would graduate.

The men really began signing up for school after that. Redneck told them, "We all know if I can pass, everyone can!" He gave the men hope, and he encouraged others. Redneck went on from glory to glory, subject by subject, passing every test.

His last test was reading. When he hit the submit button on the test and it showed he passed, he couldn't even move. He sat with his head between his hands and sobbed. When he finally came out, he looked at me and said, "Thank you for believing in me. No one has ever encouraged me or done anything for me in the past. I sure appreciate you."

When he graduated, I told Redneck that I had chosen him to become a tutor in the school. He was filled with pride that day as he introduced me to his brother and sister-in-law.

Redneck is serving life without parole. He said that he was protecting his daughter from a man who was going to hurt her. They got in a fight, Redneck fired a gun, and the man died. I have witnessed that protective nature firsthand. At the first orientation after graduation, all four of my tutors attended. At that time, Redneck stood up and told the men, "I don't care how mad you get at me, but if you ever touch Beth, you will regret it. I may be on crutches, but I can move fast. No one here will ever harm her."

FLO

With the prison school steadily growing, I needed more tutors to keep up with all of my students. I now had forty-eight students, quadruple the number I had had at the start of my work in the Walls. Along with Shooter, Shorty, and Redneck, Flo became one of my tutors.

Flo's story was just as unique as those of my other tutors. Flo was a slim black man, six feet seven tall. He was reportedly head of one of the biggest black gangs in the prison, and he was serving a double life sentence for murdering two people in a car. He'd been sitting in the backseat when a drug deal went bad, and he killed both people in the front seat. He shared this with me after we had known each other for a while, but in my eyes, he was just a good student.

Flo and I got along well. He understood my no-tolerance policy for gang activity in the school. He really tried to comply. Some days, he would come to work looking exhausted. Before I left, he told me he needed me to keep him straight. He knew I didn't put up with inmates feeling sorry for themselves and, if they did something wrong, I was the first to call them on it. I knew that would help them stay on the best path, and along with many others like him, Flo did his best to do right by me.

Still, while Flo was in school, he ended up in the hole a couple of times. He was a supposed gang leader, and whatever his position in the prison, he occasionally took the fall for the activity of some of the men who looked up to him. Every time I paid Flo a surprise visit in the hole, however, I saw math lying out all over his bed. He wanted to understand it, but math was his kryptonite. I would go to lockup and hold classes for him and a couple of others who were close to graduating.

All the other subjects were so easy for Flo, but when it came time for him to make his first attempt at the math test, he failed. He didn't finish in the time allowed. I knew he was ready for the test. He failed because he lacked confidence, not knowledge. I knew I had to figure out a different path to success for him.

That day, as I left the prison at about 4 p.m., I called my daughter and told her I was going to the track to walk and think things through. I liked going there because it was a good distraction and it helped me think. Around 7:15, my phone rang. It was my husband, wondering where I was. I explained I was at the track.

He was stunned. "Look, Beth. It's dark outside. You've been at the track for over three hours." I was surprised. I hadn't realized so much time had passed because my mind was going round and round, trying to figure out how to help Flo pass his test.

Flo's problem wasn't unfamiliar to me. The biggest challenge with many of my students was a lack of confidence. I was sure Flo knew his material, but he wouldn't allow himself to relax enough to take the test. Then I had an idea. The next day, I pulled Shorty and Shooter to the side to enlist their help. They were in, and I said they had to go along with what I said because Flo would believe it more if we all agreed.

When Flo walked into class, I told him straight out that he was going to test the next day.

"No way," he said. "I'll fail!"

"No, you won't," I told him. "I have a solution."

"Wait till you hear this one," Shorty chimed in.

"This will work," Shooter added.

I told Flo that when he got his test, he needed to pick his favorite letter. "Go through the entire test and put that letter in as your answer," I said. "Once you have done that, you no longer need to worry about having enough time to finish the test. You're finished! Now you can relax and just take the test."

Our strategy worked. The next day, Flo relaxed. He finished his test with twenty minutes to spare, and he earned a ten on it when he only needed an eight. When he came out, he gave me a big hug, which was against rules, but he was so happy, and I knew that the officers reviewing the footage on the cameras would understand. He told me when he had picked his first letters, he chose "B" as his lucky letter. "B for Beth," he said. He squatted down and sat for a bit, wiping tears from his eyes. Later, the tutors and I told him how we had strategized to help him relax during the test. The treatment director announced at graduation that Flo would become a tutor. When we came back to class after graduation, Flo was sitting in my classroom working with a couple of students. I was doing math problems on the board when I heard Flo. He looked over at the student next to him and said, "Man, you gotta multiply first. You have to follow the order of operations. Let me show you."

I didn't say anything. I just smiled. The next day, I was again working a problem, when I heard Flo say, "Man, listen, when you multiply you have to add the exponents, not subtract them. That's when you divide."

I stopped class and smiled at Flo. He smiled back. I shook my head at him. "Where was this guy when it was time to test?" I teased. "Listen to yourself. You got this!"

He beamed. "It's easy now," he admitted. Now that he didn't have to take a test anymore, everything he studied and learned just clicked, and it all seemed so simple. He looked at the student he was working with and said, "Man, you are going to pass this test, and I am going to help you. No worries."

Flo, I thought, shaking my head. *You gave me gray hair for nothing*!

Sadly, Flo's story during the time I worked at the prison did not have a happy ending. In July, about a month before I left the prison for a new position, there was a small riot. It lasted for only about a minute, but it involved approximately eighty offenders fighting in the yard. No officers were involved, but when the camera footage was reviewed, it appeared that Flo had been the one who had started the fight. I could see that he had probably incited the riot. However, I also noticed that when an offender approached a guard, Flo instructed him to lie down. He ordered others to lie down too, indicating the fight was over. Despite this, everyone involved had to be locked down for a month. Many major and minor reports needed to be written, and it took a very long time for security to figure out who all needed to be disciplined.

Due to his involvement, however, Flo was locked up with everyone else, and his tutoring days were over. He had forfeited his right to a position in the school. I visited Flo before I left the prison for my new job. He told me that he stopped the offender from hurting the guard because he wanted to do the right thing as I was always encouraging him to do. It was sad to me that the gang life's hold on Flo was too strong for him to remember this all the time.

JACKS

Fights were part of prison life. Right before I started teaching there, several men, including Jacks, a tall black man sporting dreads, got in a fight in the school. Rumor has it that he and the offender with whom he was fighting really made a mess of the classroom. Despite the rumors, Jacks and I always got along fine, though he did have a little attitude. All it took to win him over was a few pointed compliments in front of the other students. I simply shared with the classroom the truth that I was impressed with Jacks's math skills.

Jacks was always in his underwear when I went to see him. I would bang on his door, announce I was there, and give him a minute before looking through the window. But despite this, whenever I looked, he was always still there in his underwear. He also had no problem sitting on the toilet while having a conversation with me. That seemed natural for all of them; their privacy had been stripped away long ago.

I began to believe that Jacks purposely took off his pants when I came by, and so I just stopped looking in his window. I still brought him work, though. My goal was for him to graduate, and so I had to let the rest of it go. If you aren't thick skinned, you can't work in a prison, period. One time, when I walked away, I could hear Jacks tell the cellie next to him, "I bet she likes my bulge more than yours." I just kept walking.

I was determined to make a difference. My students had potential, and I was going to help them reach it. I was not going to back down from my job. All their inappropriate comments just served as further evidence to me of how much I was needed. My students didn't just need to learn the subjects I had to teach. Some needed to learn how to act appropriately, and I was going to make sure they did so.

I also tried to make allowances. Many of the inmates I worked with never saw women in civilian clothes outside of tours, and few could actually converse with women at that time. They associated with some other female employees, but as the teacher at the school, I was the woman my students spent the most time with. We talked, and I got to know their behaviors and personalities quite well, probably better than anyone else in the prison. I understood how much they needed to learn and that much of the behavior that I might find objectionable was nothing personal toward me.

Rogs

Each morning as I walked across the yard to the building that contained the prison school, some of the men would call to me. As I mentioned before, prisons are extremely loud. The men didn't address me only because I'm a woman. The men in prison never have anyone to talk to, and so they want attention—everyone from Unit One on up.

The majority of the time, when the men were transferred out of maximum security, it was for good reasons—because they were going home soon or their behavior had improved enough to afford them greater privileges. There are lifers in both minimum and medium security prisons. Everything depends on an inmate's behavior. If someone killed fifty people yet doesn't cause any problems in prison, he can earn the same privileges as someone who never pulled a trigger.

Even those men I did not work with directly got to know me after a time. When I entered the yard, most of the men in the chow hall just stared. Some other men headed for breakfast and walked along the sidewalk with me. Usually, they were friendly. Some called me "Michigan," and many shouted to me from across the lawn. I earned their respect through my work and my reputation, and as that happened, more men began speaking to me and sharing their stories.

Rogs was one of the men who was slower to open up. Because he was under twenty-one, he was required to be in school, and he hated it. I learned quickly that the only person who mattered to him was his grandmother, who took care of him as a child. Rogs had already been in and out of prison twice. His schedule was such that he had to eat his lunches at school, but he would get mad because the lunches arrived at 10:30, and he didn't get to school until 11:00, so his food was always cold. He also got upset when fried chicken was served in the chow hall because, for some reason, on those days, the men who ate their lunches in school were initially served something else. My officer put an end to that because it truly wasn't fair to my students. They wanted their chicken too.

However, there was nothing I could do about Rogs's overall schedule or his early meal delivery. But Rogs couldn't let it go. He was a total jerk just about every day over the lunches being either too cold, too light, or food he didn't like.

I have to be honest here. Even teachers can snap. I vividly remember the day Rogs was to take his math test. The former teacher, Erin, was in another room preparing the tests on the computers for the men. She didn't teach anymore, allowing me to take over full duties for the school, but she still helped with testing. It was midday, and once again, right on cue, Rogs was complaining about the food. Erin heard him and cut loose on him, just screaming, "If you don't like the fucking food, I really don't care! Just shut the fuck up."

Rogs responded by telling Erin that he didn't want to test.

"Then don't take the fucking test. I don't give a fuck," Erin said. She stormed out.

Rogs was very young, and I knew the only thing that mattered to him was making his grandma proud. I also knew that since he had just been embarrassed in front of all the men, he would have to put on a show. The tutors immediately walked over by me, and Shorty warned me now wasn't the time to speak.

"Just let him settle down," he said.

I ignored him. "I agree with you. The food sucked today," I told Rogs. "But now I am starving, so I am going to eat and not complain."

Erin stuck her head in. "Testing is set up and ready for the guys," she said. Everyone got up and headed in for testing except Rogs.

Before he had a chance to say anything, I ordered him to get his butt up. "You are taking this test," I said. "We worked as a team to prepare for this test so you would all pass. You are not letting your team down." He started to speak, but I cut him off. "You have the best chance of everyone testing today to pass. I pay attention, even when you show me a little attitude. You know this. I don't call you out in front of the guys. You told me this would mean something to your grandma. Let's go pass the test!"

Shorty and Shooter shook his hand and wished him luck. Each said, "You got this, man."

I walked over to the testing room, informed Erin that Rogs would be testing today, and asked where she would like him to sit.

Rogs had ninety minutes to finish the math test, but he took it in twenty minutes. He needed an eight to pass and scored a ten. As I walked back over to my room, he thanked me. The tutors congratulated him, and I told him to go relax. Only one more test, and he would be done.

I realized I may have been a little harsh with Rogs. I was still a little ticked off with him from the week before. I had had to kick his butt out of school over his behavior regarding his meals (what else?). He called me a "fucking bitch" as he walked down the hallway. As I said, even teachers reach a boiling point. Rogs could be difficult, but I knew there was more to his story.

He never spoke of his parents and he was quite young, only nineteen. He was going home soon. I could have written him up over his storm out and insults, but I knew a write-up would only extend his stay. It wouldn't help anyone. So, instead, I had gone to his unit to speak with him. He didn't want to talk to me. He had to put on a show for the other men. Again, I wasn't having it.

I did not call him out in front of the other guys. Instead, I had an officer bring him to a side room. He called me every name in the book on the way there. The officer told him to settle down, and then the officer told me Rogs didn't want to talk to me. He said Rogs was really worked up. I told the officer I hadn't asked if he wanted to talk to me. I wanted to talk to him. The officer smiled and took me to the room.

I looked at Rogs and said, "Quit being a jerk. You are almost done with school, and so I'm not giving you a major report. I'm giving you a pass so you can go to the chow hall to eat before class tomorrow. Here is your pass. Report directly to class when you are done." I started walking out. Then I turned, looked at him, and said, "You are going to make your grandma proud."

Then I left.

Rogs showed up for class the next day.

"Rogs," I said. "We are just getting started, on page seventy-nine." He sat down and opened his packet.

When I learned what was meaningful to my students, I got the leverage I needed to help them succeed. Sometimes, we all need to be reminded of what is important in our lives because it motivates us to move forward.

Rogs completed his math course and had only social studies left to complete, but he transferred to another facility right before completing his last test. He was set, but the prison went into lockdown, and he was transferred before lockdown was over. I believe he did go on to make his grandma proud. I hope he did.

Mac

A teacher learns early not to argue with students, no matter what their age. It is a waste of time, and it causes more frustrations and problems than just ending a discussion. Sometimes, though, you get a student who tries to argue anyway. Offender Mac was one who liked to argue.

Mac, a small and skinny young black man from Africa, was well spoken and smart, but he strongly disliked women, including me. He called me racist. It was very apparent he was not going to have a white woman telling him what to do. He never asked for help from me in class but instead turned to the tutors and asked for their help.

Although he was always respectful to the men, every time he did poorly on an assignment, he blamed me. He would say, "Beth, you never taught us this. You don't know what you're doing."

My other students disagreed with him, sometimes very vocally. They knew I always covered the material. Mac just didn't study. He would argue with them and more with me. Finally, I decided I wasn't having it. Mac's attitude was beginning to affect the other students. Sometimes, I had to kick Mac out of school and send him back to his cell for his rudeness or write minor reports because he had yelled at me or called me crazy.

Mac would threaten me and refuse to do any work. Finally, he ended up getting in a fight outside of school, and he was sent to lockup for a while. Three minor reports results in a major report, which leads to time in the hole. In addition, if the offender received those reports over a short enough time period, they could receive a major report that would move him back on the tier.

After Mac got out of lockup, the men told me that he wanted to come back to school. I replied that I hoped he did. I never referred to the unpleasantness before, but I soon heard that Mac was spreading rumors that I would not allow him to come to school. After hearing this, I made an appointment to personally invite him back to class in a way he could understand and respect. I had my opportunity one day, a day when I saw Mac walk into the program's building, then head toward the yard.

I approached him and said, "There's an orientation coming up in two weeks, and I expect you to be there. You are very well spoken and smart. Your name should already be on the wall. If you don't want to help yourself, come help other guys."

I turned and walked away without giving him a chance to speak. Two weeks later, he walked into Door Seven for orientation. I smiled and said, "It is good to see you, Mr. Mac."

Mac never did care for me, so I was surprised when he thanked me in his graduation speech. He gave the tutors much credit for their patience with him, and they did indeed deserve his recognition. He shared how prison time had allowed him to reflect on his life, and he was using the time to think about what he had done and how he could be a better person.

I learned that he was in prison for mugging and murdering two women. The women had not resisted his attempt to rob them, handing over their purses immediately when he demanded them. But his hatred of women had grown over the years, and he was still very young. When Mac entered my classroom, he was only twenty-one and had a lot more growing up to do, but I do believe I saw the start of some of that growth over his time in the prison school.

T. M.

I had model students and difficult students, and occasionally I encountered inmates in the Walls who didn't even come to the school but nevertheless respected what I was doing. One such was T. M., an elderly inmate who worked in the school and chapel areas, doing the cleaning. He had received a life sentence after killing someone while already in prison. He was extremely intelligent, and the officers and other students told me he knew all the laws. He acted as an attorney in the Walls for the men, researching and helping them with their cases. What they did for him in return, I do not know.

Not many people seemed to like him, and they called him Sticky Fingers because he would steal anything he could get his hands on. But he was an ardent writer, and I wanted to encourage that. I gave him pencils and paper whenever he needed them, so he was always respectful to me.

I can recall his last day in the prison, when he was transferring to another one. He came down to the school to talk to me. He said that he knew he would be transferred soon, and he wanted to warn me that an offender by the name of Wasp had been trying to get to me for months. He said he had been paying close attention to him and started noticing that Wasp was following me and coming down by the classroom. Wasp also cleaned in the building, and so he was around a lot. T. M. said, "I respect you, Beth. You didn't ask me to look out for you, but I wanted to. I am leaving now, and the men know to keep an eye on Wasp. He won't get to you, but I still wanted you to know. Just be careful."

Although Wasp was already being watched, I still needed to tell Officer Dan immediately. I talked to my tutors as well. Shorty had realized the potential threat long ago, and he was handling it on his own. He mentioned to me that he would observe Wasp standing by the chow hall window and watching me walk down the sidewalk every morning. Shorty made sure to never leave work until I was ready to walk down the hall and outside. I hadn't realized he was waiting to make sure I was safe. I thought he was just putting off heading back to the cell house. Shorty explained that I was usually the last person in the hall for the day, and although I was on camera, he still didn't think it would be good for me to walk out alone. Because of T. M.'s warning, I was able to be more mindful of my safety and take necessary precautions.

REY

As our program grew, other civilians who worked in the prison took notice. A yoga instructor who came in from New York for a week to teach the men used one of the classrooms. She told Officer Dan how she walked by the school every day and was so impressed. She said she had not seen a school so organized in all the time she spent in prisons; the men were on task all the time! Hearing this kind of evaluation from someone from the outside meant a lot to all of us.

However, despite all the growth I witnessed in my time in the Walls and all the lives I flatter myself to believe I helped change, it is certainly unrealistic to say I reached all my students. There were some whom I could not help, as is the case for any teacher.

Rey was one of those men. In the twenty-five years he'd been attending school, he hadn't improved. I don't say this very often, but I truly felt he was at the limit for his potential to learn. I didn't even understand what he was saying most of the time. If I was talking about history, he would start talking about aliens or topics that weren't even close to the discussion the rest of us were having. Although he really tried, he needed to take some time off.

Inspired by Redneck, many new students were enrolling, and school really filled up quickly. Redneck gave them all hope, and so I told Rey, who was showing no progression, to take a break in order to open a spot for another student. In doing so, I told him if we offered any new educational classes, he would be welcome to attend. I made sure Officer Dan accompanied me when I gave Rey the news. I had mixed feelings. I didn't want to turn anyone away, but others who hadn't had the opportunities Rey did wanted in.

He was furious and said that it wasn't fair that he couldn't go to school. He even challenged me, saying, "How can you be a teacher and still need to look up things about history?" He didn't or wouldn't understand that my background was in mathematics.

TRAGEDIES OUTSIDE DOOR SEVEN

Sometimes the stories I heard about what my students did outside of school, or once they were released from prison, were sad or even disturbing. One man, Games, was always in and out of lockup because of his frequent sexual encounters with other offenders. The first month I was there, he said he was going to the chapel to get some papers. When he didn't return, the CERT team went looking for him and found him in a closet with another offender. When in school, he was always respectful. He struggled to read but was working hard to improve. But as I watched him working, I couldn't help but wonder, *Does he know right from wrong? Is he a threat to society?*

I did not understand the phrase "gay for the stay" until I worked in the prison. Even straight men would engage in sexual activities, I found, because they had no other outlet. For a time, my students hoped the prison would consider conjugal visits to help deal with this issue, but as of the writing of this book, nothing has been done.

I worried about students like Quiet in the harsh environment of the prison. He was under twenty-one, but he was serving a life sentence. Supposedly, he hurt his girlfriend and locked her in the bathroom. His parents took the girl to the hospital, but then she pressed charges for kidnapping and attempted murder.

Quiet struck me as being too young to deal with prison life. He was shy yet respectful. His parents visited him every week. He was scared, and I could see it in his eyes and actions. He always asked if he could stay and eat lunch in the back room and study because he didn't want to go to the chow hall. The other students got wind of it and started taking him to lunch, which gave me some relief, yet I always worried that someday he might harm himself. I worried prison would be too much for him because he seemed just like a quiet little boy, trying to find a way to stay alive.

Dannport, a six feet seven black man in his thirties, loved to talk about his daughter. He missed her so much. He had been in and out of prison for various crimes over the years, and I worked with him at the old prison while the men were on lockdown. I would go over and teach him math in an attempt to get him to finish his schooling before he was paroled. He had only six weeks to go, and he was grateful I took the time to walk over to his cell each day and work with him. The conversation was an added bonus, during lockdown. I made it a point to talk to the men in the cells next to Dannport too.

Unfortunately, Dannport did not finish his math course before the first time he left the prison. Even more unfortunately, when he had been out in the world just a month, he got into a confrontation with an officer. He ended up back in prison for a short term, just long enough to earn his diploma. He never thought he would graduate because math frustrated him. He worked so hard and struggled so much to pass it, but pass it he did, and the second time he left the Walls, he went home a graduate.

But as much as I value education, it is not a cure-all. A few weeks after Dannport left prison, his body was found floating in a river. His death was ruled an accident.

Purcy, a twenty-year-old white man, was another whose life came to a very sad end. He was extremely smart and went through the program quite quickly. I could tell he enjoyed coming to school, and he asked if he could continue coming after graduation. According to the school rules, he could not. He wanted to somehow find a way to help others, and so I suggested he help those studying in the pods. A few weeks after he graduated, he returned home. Only a few months later he was found dead, victim of a stabbing.

ROCKO

Some of my students touched my heart and soul in a way I will never forget. Rocko was one of them. A tall black man in his twenties, Rocko was very respectful to me. One day, he came to class seeming really down, as well as a bit angry. Because I had never had difficulty with him before, I asked him to stay after class that morning to talk. He was scheduled to take a test in the afternoon, and something just wasn't right with him.

When Rocko stayed after, I asked the tutors to go to another room so I could talk to him alone. I could see the sadness in his eyes. "Okay," I said. "Please talk to me. I know something's wrong."

He looked directly at me and said, "My girl committed suicide today. It happens. There isn't anything I can do."

"Rocko, it's okay to cry," I told him.

He shook his head. "No. Not in front of the men."

"Men cry in front of me all the time," I said.

"Sure, when they pass a test."

"No," I told him. "When they need to. It is okay."

A few tears came down his cheeks, and as he wiped them away, he told me he would be all right.

"You don't need to test today," I told him. "Go and take some time for yourself."

He appreciated that, and I told him when he was ready, I would have him signed up to test. I also warned him not to get into a fight that night, not to blame himself or take out his anger on others. We agreed he should just remember the good times with her.

The next morning, he did not come to class, and so at count, I went to check on him. I walked up to his door, pounded on it, and said, "Rocko, it's Beth."

He came to the door, and we talked. "Tell me a story about your girl," I said.

He talked about how he loved to go for walks with her, holding her hand and laughing.

"You really care," he said.

I told him I cared about all my students.

"I didn't come to see you because I wanted you back in school," I said. "I hope to learn more about her because then I also learn about you."

He came back to school that afternoon.

I thanked him for working hard, for not giving up, for staying focused, and for caring about himself.

COLES

I had one conversation with an inmate I will never forget. Coles, a young black nineteen-year-old, had dreads that he twisted constantly. When he started school, I couldn't help noticing his negative attitude and feared he wouldn't do well. He ended up attending one of the prison reform classes, and when he came back from that class, he had a completely different attitude. He wanted to learn, and he wanted to graduate.

One day, he arrived at school a couple of minutes before the other men. "Beth, how old are you?" he asked.

"How old do you think I am?"

He looked at me and said, "Thirty-six or thirty-seven?"

I laughed and said, "Try forty-seven."

His eyes got huge. "Beth, you're old!" he said. "You've lived a long life. I've never known anyone who lived that long, so far. Me and my homies will never live to forty-seven."

I realized he wasn't joking. I could feel my eyes begin to tear up, so I quickly grabbed a tissue, got up from my desk, and started to walk to the back of the room. I didn't want to show my emotions in front of him, and I told him I was looking for a book for him.

I couldn't help but think about how differently I had been raised compared my students. The disparities stunned me. Sometimes, I would drive home with tears in my eyes, thinking of all the men, both young and old, who would die in prison. Most of them had deserved their sentences when they were handed down, but I could see the scared little boy in so many of them. I could see how they had no direction in life. They needed to learn to use appropriate language, how to accept failures, and how to be kind. Many of these men came from nothing, had nothing. They didn't have anyone to love them and spent their lives dodging bullets. So many of them didn't know the simple joy of playing a board game or sharing a family holiday dinner because they were too busy trying to survive. My interaction with Coles and my experience within the Walls gave me a new appreciation for life and inspired me to even work harder to help these men be successful. They didn't have any idea what success felt like. Many didn't know how it felt to truly live at all.

I told the men, "A simple compliment can mean so much to someone. If you have a chance to give one, don't pass it up. You may change someone's attitude for the better." I worked with them on teamwork with different and sometimes difficult people, perhaps rival gang members, and with people of different culture and skin color, including me.

MAY

Several of my students said that racism was rampant in the prison. In fact, one of the biggest concerns the men had about me from the beginning was whether I was racist. They watched everything I did, and I would hear them asking each other if they thought I was a bigot or a racist.

But as I treated all my students with the same respect, day after day, they took notice. I gained a lot of respect in their eyes by dealing fairly with everyone. They began to open up about their experiences.

The courts were racist, they said, and nobody cared about them because they didn't have money or they were the wrong color. White men, they said, were only in prison if they were poor. "Look around the room," they often challenged me. "How many white people are in school?"

For a long time, I ignored what the men told me. They all started school with negative attitudes, complaining about almost everything. But as school progressed, they stopped talking about race, and when that happened, I started to pay more attention. I can remember looking around my classroom one day and noticing that I had only two white students. The majority *were* black or Latino. *Why is that*? I wondered. Why did the men talk so much about race? When something didn't go the way a student wanted it to, right away I was called a racist. I just shook it off, knowing in my heart who I was. Eventually, the men knew it too, and they stopped using race as an excuse.

I then noticed how when new students would come in and try to play the racist card, the other men would step up and say, "No, she's not a racist. You just need to do your work and quit blaming her for your lack of effort."

The men went to great lengths to ensure they had my back on this issue.

Sometimes they went too far. I had a student in his early twenties called May. He was very skinny and always had a smile on his face. He really did try hard in school, but he was always three problems behind the rest of us. Every time I completed a math problem with the class, I would step aside and ask the men some questions about it. Then I would ask if anyone wanted me to redo the problem.

Well, two problems later, May's hand would go up, and he would say, "Could we go back a few problems?"

This behavior was constant. I tried to be patient, but the other students were getting irritated. One day, I left the room to get copies.

May was hurt because I was occasionally frustrated with him. The men assured him I wasn't racist, and then, in an attempt to get him to shut up and quit focusing on that, they told him I was married to a black man.

I didn't realize what had happened at first. I found out only later, after May left the prison. But from that day on, May never said a bad thing about me.

I was a little disappointed when he left. He hadn't had time to finish his degree. He had started late and hadn't had time to complete all the tests in the six weeks he had had in school. On his last day, I told him I was going to miss him. He smiled and said, "Really, I will miss you too. You're not racist, Beth. I thought you were for a while, but you aren't." He said he was excited for his sister to pick him up.

Later, when the men told me what they had done that day I left the classroom, my feelings were mixed. I didn't like that all the men had made up and gone along with a lie, but after thinking about it, I thought it was pretty awesome that they were taking care of me. They truly knew I wasn't racist and wanted May to see that in me as well. He had to if he was ever going to get past it and concentrate on learning.

CALLER

My students also began defending me from racism charges on the yard. They would not tolerate the negativity. On the yard, they told everyone to back off the subject. They realized I just wanted to help as many of them as possible get an education.

One time, I heard from Officer Dan that one of my former students, Caller, had just completed his time in lockup and wanted to come back to school.

With so many men coming and going, I had difficulty remembering Caller at first, even though he had been attending school for three months or so prior to being thrown into lockup. Officer Dan said he was a tall black man in his late twenties with a stocky build.

I kept telling Dan, "I know who you are talking about, but I don't think he is black."

Dan and the tutors looked at me strangely. "You're thinking of someone else," Dan said. "He's black."

"I know exactly who you're talking about because he was a pain in the butt, always whining and complaining, but I'm still not going to deny him an education."

Officer Dan and my tutors agreed that Caller was a pain but assured me he was indeed black. We ended up looking at his picture on the computer because I would not agree. Of course they were right, and I was wrong.

"Well, I just don't care about the color of skin. I care about work ethics and attitudes," I said defensively. This shocked them all, but I knew they believed me. The incident ended up spreading through the prison like wildfire. The men finally had proof, once and for all, that I looked at all my students for who they were on the inside, not the color of their skin on the outside. Caller had just completed his time in lockup and he wanted to attend school again.

7

Graduation

"The direction in which education starts a man,
will determine his future."
—**Plato**

During the years I worked at the prison, I had the honor of presiding over the largest single-year graduation ceremony held in maximum security on record. There were a total of seventeen graduates. The year before, there had been seven. The incredible growth I had witnessed in the prison school program reinforced for me that the innovations I had implemented were truly a success. The men responded to a well-organized, more traditional-type school setting, including class discussions, competitions, and a teacher who truly believed in them, without judgment.

In attendance graduation day were the warden, deputy warden, security warden, treatment director, school officer, counselors, the president of the college that offered the school program, CERT team members, psychiatrists, other employees, and some of the inmates' family members. Also in attendance was a team of filmmakers who were making a documentary on a graduate. The bishop of the Davenport Diocese, who was close with that same graduate, attended as a special guest.

As the students prepared for the ceremony, they were full of nerves, knowing they would soon get up to give a speech in front of the attendees, something they had never done in their lives. I walked around and spoke to each graduate. Some were being interviewed by the local news, while others congregated, nervously talking to each other, excited for this day most never expected would happen in their lifetimes. Wearing their red caps and gown, the men stood tall.

I tried to express to them the importance of being recognized that day. "When you do something positive, allow others to take notice. Be proud. Exposing your good side will only help those trying to fight for change become more inspired. Even if you aren't getting out, people in this world need to see what happens in prisons and how people can earn a diploma and turn their lives around."

Many of the graduates were scared to speak with the editor from the newspaper; however, none turned the editor down after I expressed to them that the editor was writing positive news. Then I had too many wanting to speak! Many of my students had had negative experience with the press due to their past crimes. Now they couldn't believe there was something positive the paper had to report.

Barbs was one student who had particular trouble accepting positive attention. He had trouble accepting love and care, even on the best of terms. He once shared with me how his brother's adoptive parents had offered to take him in as well. He lived with them for a while because they had a huge home, and he had his own space in a beautifully remodeled basement. His brother's parents were doctors, and they had strong family values, saying, "I love you," to each other and eating as a family. Barbs admitted that was just too much love for him. It made him uncomfortable because he had never experienced that kind of care as a kid. He was so uncomfortable not only because of all the love but because they were educated and he was not. Although he admired them and cared for them, he chose not to stay with them, instead getting into trouble out on the streets.

Now Barbs, a short, stocky black man with dreads, was in his late twenties, one of the barbers in the prison. He had transferred from another prison with two classes left to complete in his school course: math and reading. He had finished them in our classroom, and now he would have the honor of walking in our ceremony. He had told me how he wanted to invite his brother's adoptive mom, the woman he called his second mom, to his graduation.

But a few weeks before the ceremony, he came to me and confided that he had lied to his family in his previous prison, telling them he had already graduated.

I told him not to worry about that because when you transfer, sometimes you miss the graduation ceremony and can choose to attend at another prison. I told him he could tell his family that this is what had happened in his case. He looked at me, his eyes wide with shock, and said, "You would do that for me?"

I said I didn't see how a little lie would hurt anything, and I told him to get back to work and graduate so his mom could come to the graduation.

The graduation ceremonies were held in the visiting room, and a list of graduates was posted by the door in a decorative fashion. The prison was serving a graduation cake, fruit punch, nuts, and cookies. On the wall were a couple of small graduation posters. The graduates proudly walked in one by one to "Pomp and Circumstance" with big smiles on their faces. The warden spoke first, and the president of the college that employed me handed out diplomas to each graduate. The graduates then each had a turn to speak, and I remember the entire wonderful day.

Although I was told by the coordinator to speak for only ten minutes, I ended up taking forty-five. I needed every bit of that extra time to let the men know the significance of their achievements and to give each one the accolades they were due. This day was supposed to be extra special for these men, and I made it my job to ensure that it was. It was so important to me that my students had a meaningful graduation, and I really wanted them to understand what a huge step forward they had made in earning their diplomas. In my speech, I urged them to look to the future, beyond this huge success, and contemplate what they would accomplish next. I told them to move forward and not look back.

I spoke of the challenges all the men encountered. I spoke of their successes and failures. Most importantly, I told each of my students just how proud I was of them. I told them how awesome it was that they continued on with a strong work ethic to make their dream of graduation come true. I praised them because each one had come to me, asking which student they could help next. To me, that meant more than anything else. They now wanted to give back, and instead of thinking only of themselves, they were encouraging each other and wanting to make a difference in someone else's life. To me, this change was monumental.

"Look around," I told them. "You all have something in common. You came to class daily, you worked hard, you became part of a team, you failed together and succeeded together, you cared about your classmates, and most importantly, when times were tough, you never gave up. I believed in you, and you believed in yourselves. Look at the officers and counselors. These men and women believed in you too. Many times, I heard how they helped you in the pods. This amazing team came together to help you succeed. Your families and friends contributed as well. You wanted to show them that you could succeed. I know many of you were on the phone with them after passing a test because you knew how proud they would be of you. Thank you, everyone in this room, for being an inspiration to our graduates."

I also spoke about Flo and Shorty, the Adult National Honor Society students who were inducted at graduation. They shared a strong work ethic. Each one put in much time and effort and worked hard to accomplish their goals. For one of them, math was his kryptonite, and for the other, writing, because English was his second language. Yet they both persevered.

Then it was the graduates' turn to speak. Shorty's speech was especially moving because he delivered it in Spanish for his mother, who did not speak English, and it was translated by his cellmate and cotutor, Shooter. "I am not only graduating today, but I'm also a tutor for the education program," he said. "First and foremost, I would like to thank God for giving me the knowledge and opening my eyes to be able to see how important education is. I never imagined that I would be standing here today, receiving my diploma." He thanked the officers who supported him, as well as the former warden and the bishop. He then thanked me. Finally, he said, "I would like to take this opportunity to share with you how education has changed my life. Being able to read and write has allowed me to understand life much better and stay up on today's news. Learning math has given me the opportunity to become a tutor in school. I love doing math and being able to help others with it. I see their struggles and understand their difficulties. The math we do is advanced and brings out a lot of emotion in all of us. Many students needed to follow our school motto: 'Eat, Sleep, Math' to be successful. There were days when students just wanted to give up and walk away, but as you can see by the number of graduates we have here today, those students didn't just give up. We always knew that each day may be hard, but tomorrow was another day to pick ourselves up and try again. I never thought in my life that I would be standing in front of a group of students, teaching math problems or working on science problems to students that only speak English, but now I know that hard work truly pays off. I have learned so much about life from school.

"One of the most important things I have learned from my teacher is the power of a compliment. Beth would say, 'You don't need to buy someone a gift to make them happy. Perhaps just telling them that they worked hard today or that they did a great job on a test or just saying good morning with an honest smile can make a big difference in someone's life,' and this is true. I have witnessed this with my own eyes."

Redneck spoke next. "In January, I was at a fifth-grade reading level and a lower level in mathematics. Today, my educational level is twelfth grade. To me, this is amazing. I could not have accomplished this on my own. I never cared about my education until one day when my child asked me a math question for a school assignment and I could not answer. I was so sad, being a fifty-year-old man and not being able to answer a simple question for my child. That is when I realized it was time to get educated. The more I learned, the better I felt. Students started asking me for help, and it was a great feeling, not only knowing the answers but being able to help others. I want to pass my knowledge on to others and encourage them to work hard."

Kinsy said, "Education is so valuable. Today, we need education to communicate with others and make a living. As a teenager, I chose to run the streets with the wrong crowd instead of attending school. In order to pass to the seventh grade, I had to attend summer camp. I was thirteen years old and in the sixth grade, and this was not because I couldn't do the work. It was because I chose not to do it. I thought I was being cool at the time. I now realize the cool kids were the ones that were learning and willing to learn. Because of my age, I thought I was too old to graduate, and so I never attended high school. And so, with that said, I want to thank this educational program for allowing me to earn my diploma. I also want to thank Beth, Shooter, and Shorty for working with me and most of all believing in me when I doubted myself. You can either be your worst enemy or your own role model. We are all role models today. Keep finishing whatever it is that you start. We all started school, and look where we are today. Keep moving forward. Thank you, and God Bless."

My other wonderful tutor, Shooter, had already graduated. He did not give a speech, but the men he had helped got together and wrote a tribute to him, which Flo read.

"Shooter came to prison as a kid always in trouble. He had to grow up in prison, and that is exactly what happened. He began to learn from his mistakes and think differently about life . . . He started appreciating life and decided to write a book about his own life. He wrote about his struggles to get to America and how life was so much worse back home. He spoke about how much appreciation he has for the meals, clothes, and shelter he has been given. Since Shooter has such a desire to learn, working in the school as a tutor has given him the opportunity to spread his passion. Although he is willing to help in all the subject areas, his passion is teaching writing. He makes classes more interesting with his witty personality, and he never leaves any student behind. Together, we discuss each other's difficulties, and he encourages us to learn from each other. Working with Shooter in school, students learn quickly that his only goal is for each and every student to succeed. He wants everyone to better himself through knowledge. His patience, compassion, and dedication show how selfless he is. When he is in the yard, he takes the time to ask us if we have completed our homework and offers to help. He is more than willing to give up his yard time to help us. We truly believe when he leaves prison he will spend his time as a writer, motivational speaker, or a mentor to kids. You are a true inspiration to us all, Shooter, and we thank you for your time, patience and knowledge."

The students also retold some of Shorty's story.

"Shorty spends all his time helping others and making people feel better about themselves. He always has something positive to say, and you never know if he is having a bad day because he doesn't let that change him. We hope he gets another chance at life because he will not end up back here. He will end up coaching kids, getting more education so that he can continue teaching math, helping others, however possible, enjoying his family, and being very involved in the Catholic church. His appreciation for life will open many doors for him, and we know he will make a significant difference in this world. Thank you, Shorty. We have the utmost respect for you. Keep doing what you are doing—spreading your knowledge and positive energy to everyone. We know life has more to offer you."

Flo, the other student who received the Adult National Honor Society Award, never gave up through all of his struggles. I shared with everyone how I had walked the track for hours for him, searching for solutions. Smiling, I apologized to him—and to the bishop—for how the tutors and I had tricked him at test time in order to help him relax.

When Flo spoke, he asked everyone to stand. He announced that I had been named a correctional teacher of the year. He said, "We (the graduates) want to thank you and want you to know how deserving you are of this award. You not only believed in us but treated us as humans. You never judged us or treated us as less than. You weren't afraid of us and expected us to work hard and help others. You didn't accept excuses and wouldn't allow us to feel sorry for ourselves. We are here today because of you. None of us ever had support like you have given us. Thank you for showing us that we can accomplish positive things, we are valued, and we can make a difference by helping others. You are the true definition of a teacher, and we will never forget you."

After the ceremony, the men all wanted me to meet their families. As I spent time with each of them, I quickly learned that many of their family members never had an education, and some had done "time" themselves. They were all very respectful and appreciative and eager to meet and talk with me. Barbs was so excited for me to meet his second mom that he anxiously made a beeline toward me. When he introduced her to me, right away, he said "I told her the truth. I told her I hadn't graduated at the other prison."

He looked at his mom, nodded to me, and said, "She sucked us all in. She was so sugar at the beginning, and once she got to know us, she became a hard-ass. She worked us to death." He smiled at me and said, "Thank you. If you weren't a hard-ass, I never would have finished the math class."

Rods's mother had called me the day before graduation. She said her son told her he was graduating, and she wanted me to confirm this because she didn't believe it. I told her yes, he was telling the truth. I asked her to please attend because her son would be receiving a special recognition at graduation. I had nominated him for the National Adult Education Society (NAE). When she walked in, I happened to be standing next to her son. He had the biggest smile on his face. He said with pride, "That's my mom. I haven't seen her in ten years." During the ceremony, I announced those students I was recommending for Adult National Honor Society, and when I said Rods's name, I looked at his mom in the audience. She was so proud at that moment that she stood up, clapping, with tears coming down her cheeks. I told everyone at that moment, "If you want to have a real conversation with someone about history or politics, Rods is your man. He is smart, open minded, and has a true love for history and politics."

Rods couldn't wait for the ceremony to be over. He went right to his mom and gave her a huge hug, and tears swam in both their eyes. He walked up to me afterward to formally introduce me and thank me. Then he said, "I used to be racist. I was a skinhead." His use of the past tense testified to me once again that real change is possible and gave me an incredible gift.

I was so grateful that day. My students showed me again and again how I made a difference in their lives. I saw the progress we had made together not only in the kind words they spoke of me but in their actions. They were no longer living their lives only for themselves. They were each dedicated to helping others be successful. I cried that night as I replayed the day in my mind, the speeches these men had given. I recalled how proud they were to introduce me to their family members. I thought about the men who didn't have family at the ceremony and how the other graduates invited them to join their families. I thought about Flo and Redneck and how the treatment director announced at the ceremony that they would now be tutors in the school. They stood proudly, filled with purpose.

During my time at the prison, I was fortunate enough to participate in three graduation ceremonies. Each one reinforced for me loudly and clearly how people can change, truly change, if someone believes in them. Each graduation was more incredible than the last, with more incredible things happening as more and more people got involved and became advocates for my students.

A few weeks before the last graduation ceremony I participated in within the Walls, an offender who was not even a student of mine walked up to me and asked, "Miss Beth, what is your favorite cake?"

"Chocolate," I told him.

"I like chocolate too," he said.

Although I found his behavior a little strange, I didn't give it another thought. A few days later, Officer Dan told me the offender NAACP organization would like to invite me to their next meeting. That was great. I wanted to meet with all the organizations because I wanted to form an educational club and was looking for ideas. The NAACP meetings were held in the card room at the end of the hall. My tutors, Shooter and Shorty, along with all of the graduates, were also invited. When I walked in the room, all the men stood and clapped. I was surprised and confused. They asked me to come up to their podium, and when I did, I was presented with the First Lady of Teaching Award.

One of the NAACP members spoke and shared how they had heard a lot about me and how all the men appreciated how well I treated everyone, whether they were my students or not. He spoke for a while, and then the men asked me to speak. I was again able to share how very proud I was of all the men for their work and for their efforts in school and out. I appreciated the fact that they helped each other and even in tough times kept their chins held high.

I talked about how I knew there was more to be done within the school and how being the only teacher was tough because I had so many students. I shared my goal to start the Educational Club for those who already had diplomas yet wanted to continue their education outside the classroom. I hoped to have competitions in art, history, math, and science, allowing everyone to show their creativity.

The men seemed very excited by this, and the same man spoke about Shooter and Shorty. He mentioned how much the men appreciated their patience, help, and positivity. The other NAACP members then said how we all, including Officer Dan and Officer Roy, made a great team, because we never judged anyone. They handed the tutors certificates for their hard work, and then they gave each graduate a certificate and congratulated them. The effects of positivity are far reaching. People, offenders, and organizations I didn't even know were recognizing us for our efforts. Amazing things were happening.

After the speech was over, the men served strawberry pie and ice cream. After I finished my pie, I moved from table to table, thanking each and every one for such kindness and for letting me know, once again, that I was making a difference. It meant so much to me that they truly understood who I was and what I was about—helping others reach their potential and never giving up on anyone, no matter how tough times got. The conversation that day was full of laughter and great ideas. So many men had awesome things to bring to the program. I have used some ideas in the teaching I do today, and I will continue to share these ideas with others.

But there was still one more surprise for me. The next day when I entered the classroom, on my desk was a little white box. On that box was a note. "We are sorry this wasn't ready for you yesterday. We know it is your favorite." Inside that box, I found a small chocolate cake.

8

A Voice for Those Who Can't Speak

"If you are working on something that you really care about,
you don't have to be pushed. The vision pulls you."
—Steve Jobs

As I completed my last day of work at the prison, I had many emotional conversations with offenders, both current and former students. There was much sadness that day for all of us. Many student offenders expressed to me that I was their motivation, and they didn't want to see me go. I told them that I would continue to be their motivation on the outside, as long as they continued to succeed and be better people on the inside.

Many told me that they would continue to help others and hoped someday they would be given a second chance to show the world they had changed. Those who took school seriously were now educated. They knew how to talk appropriately, show respect, care about others, and be accountable. They now saw their potential and had the confidence to succeed in life, where in the past they were not able to see a future for themselves and couldn't see themselves succeeding at anything. They had nothing to look forward to because most knew only about street life. They never held respectable jobs and were never shown how much potential they had. They knew only a life of abuse, drugs, and gangs. At school, they were taught life skills. To this day, it haunts me to remember how that nineteen-year-old student couldn't believe I had lived to the ripe old age of forty-seven. How could someone so young not know anyone who lived into their forties? That is the life many of these men led.

As I closed Door Seven, I was close to tears. I turned back and looked into the empty classroom, hoping a new teacher would come in and continue to care and not judge.

I walked down the hall with my tutors, heading out of the Walls for the last time. My tutors asked me to please go and make a difference in kids' lives, kids who could still be helped. They told me how so many kids needed role models, direction, and someone to believe in them. They truly felt I had come to the prison to show them all that there were people out there who care. They felt my time there had served a purpose and that our time together hadn't been coincidental. I felt the same way. People in prison need so badly to see that there are people in this world who care.

"We all know you have a sick daughter," Shorty said. "Yet you still came here every day to help us. When you hurt your leg, we sat in the chow hall and watched you limp down to the school. I would sit here healthy, just waiting to die, following the same routine day after day. Then you gave value to my life. You made me feel smart in front of all the other men. You believed in me, and now my family sees change in me."

Shooter said, "I don't like goodbyes. They make me want to cry. You are doing the right thing leaving. You are too good a person to be here. You are above all of this petty stuff that happens. You have class. You never treated any of us with disrespect. You did not look down on us. We all expected you to be racist, and you aren't. You were a huge surprise to us. God brought us an angel. The men talk about you being our godmother on the yard. You are our hope to leave here. You came to tell us to get educated and showed us we could accomplish anything. Some of these men have changed so much because of you. You wouldn't even begin to understand how much. You have left a positive impact on all of us. You showed these men that not everyone is looking for something. You showed these men that miracles are possible. You are our miracle. Thank you."

Shooter's words were a gift to me. He had no idea how much I felt that he and all my other students in the Walls had changed me.

As my tutors turned to head back to their pod, I continued straight toward the exit. I looked back and told the men, "You haven't heard the last of me. I will be your voice and will show the world that there are people who can change and who deserve a second chance." The men smiled sadly and waved, and I could tell how much they cared and feel their resolve to continue the work we had started.

Although my days at the prison are behind me now, I still speak frequently with Shorty and Shooter, and I write to Redneck often. Both Shorty and Shooter have transferred to other prisons, so we talk about what they are accomplishing and how proud they are to continue to help others, always thinking of ways to improve programs at their new prisons. Shooter is taking college courses, and Shorty is using his time to improve his English. He is also tutoring on his own some men who need help in math and encouraging the men to stay positive. Together, they make a list each day of the goals they want to accomplish.

Their days are busy, yet I encourage all three of them to never stop writing to politicians, thanking them for their efforts. I encourage them to tell those politicians how all the men watch the news daily in hopes of learning about second-chance opportunities after the First Step Act made so many inmates smile for the first time in years. They are now hoping reform trickles down to the states, so that everyone, not just juveniles, may earn a second chance. I share with them the good things that are happening in the justice reform movement.

Redneck is still at the prison for which I worked, and he is still tutoring in the school, helping men learn to read. He said they often ask how I am doing, and that makes me happy because it shows they still do care about others. I wish I could go back and visit them, but rules prohibit that. I am hopeful that they read this book and know how much and how often I think about them. I have not just walked away. I am keeping my promise to be a voice for justice reform, in hopes that they someday have that chance to truly live.

QUESTIONS

Until you walk in the shoes of others, you can't truly understand what they experience. As a teacher working in a maximum-security prison, I learned a new way to look at and live life and about the power of giving and receiving respect. The lesson was reinforced daily. The Seventh Door that the inmates walked through each day meant so much more to them than just a classroom. Door Seven was there for those who were ready to step into a more fulfilling season of their lives.

When I was eighteen, my ability to think and process information was at a much higher level than many of these men who are now in their thirties and older. I worked with my students in the prison school for sometimes six hours a day at a stretch, and the time I spent with them helped me realize that locking up young people—eighteen, nineteen, twenty, or even thirty years old—for life is wrong in some cases. Age is really just a number. The mentality of a person—his or her ability to reason, to think, and to learn—is what needs to be addressed.

Reforms in juvenile justice are a step in the right direction. Offering second chances to those convicted of crimes before the age of eighteen is a beautiful example of merciful and humanitarian legislation, but it does not go far enough. When are we going to stop looking at arbitrary numbers and start looking at someone's mental ability? When are we going to look at the mental ages of those who have committed crimes, how much nurturing and schooling they have actually received? Why must we focus on the number eighteen? That is not the magic number at which a person is capable of making a decision. At eighteen, is a person suddenly culpable for being raised by parents, guardians, or gang members who didn't teach them about life? Should they live their lives inside prison walls because they didn't know any better or have any better examples?

One question the men asked of me often was this: "If we have to go to school in prison until we are twenty-one, then why are we not treated in the courts as juveniles until we are twenty-one?" I didn't have an answer for them. The inequity was too glaring. Why are minors in prison adults in the courts? Shame on us, as a society, for caring only about ourselves.

I am embarrassed to say that before I came to teach in a prison, I never actually gave a thought about those incarcerated and in need of an education. These men are living examples of being "out of sight, out of mind." Perhaps politicians should begin asking psychiatrists, officers, counselors, and especially teachers what they think of these men. Once they have grown mentally, do they deserve a second chance?

I do not believe that rehabilitation is a possibility for everyone. There are offenders who need to live out their lives in prison because they socially and mentally cannot function safely in society. I am also aware that I have been personally touched and affected by the men I met in the prison and I am biased in my desire to help them. Nevertheless, I truly believe it is time we as a society take a long, hard look at substantive justice reform and begin asking ourselves the hard questions.

Isn't twenty years in prison enough for someone who has participated in a felony murder if he or she wasn't the one to pull the trigger?

Aren't twenty years enough for a person who got in a bar fight or killed someone drunk driving?

Remorse goes both ways. Many of these men have learned and feel remorse. When is it our turn?

Understandably, some victims want an eye for an eye, but how far do we carry the drive for vengeance? When is enough, enough? People make mistakes. Some people, by a twist of fate or mistake, or for whatever reason, get away with their mistakes, while others are incarcerated. If we have learned and have worked to become better people, shouldn't we rise above?

I have to point to the fact that some other countries offer a life sentence of only fifteen years. Why, in the United States, do we give so many a death sentence of life in prison, where their only chance of leaving prison is in a body bag? After ten years, I believe someone working in the prison environment has the ability to tell if an offender is capable of change. Given the right help, these people can still function well in society, but when will they get their chance?

For those capable of change and remorse, a fifteen-year sentence for the worst crimes seems to me more than adequate. After fifteen years, many offenders start losing their family and friends on the outside, and then, without that support, they have less chance of being successful in life if they are ever released. I don't believe we can continue to keep people in prison for twenty-five years and then decide to let them out with no support system. Just take a moment, imagine your life twenty-five years ago, and consider just how much has changed. The person exiting prison will walk into an entirely changed world and is most likely scared to death.

When people are given a life sentence with no chance of parole, they are forgotten about by their loved ones, friends, and society. They lose everyone who matters to them. If given a chance for parole, that hope helps them and family members continue to fight for freedom. It gives them a reason to change. Many first offenders are sitting in prison for life with no opportunity for a second chance. This needs to change.

Can you even imagine sitting in prison, under the felony murder rule, for the rest of your life because you were with someone who killed another individual?

You have culpability, but do you deserve to rot in prison for someone else's actions?

I have much respect for the politicians today who are looking at justice reform with an open mind. They realize the need to give second chances to those who have shown positive change. Understanding that offenders need more skills if they are to make it in a changed role, the Department of Corrections offers classes to help them—antiviolence courses, drug classes, Thinking for a Change, vocational classes, and more. Many offenders begin to attend church as well, and many different religions are practiced in prison.

I believe we need to start backing those politicians who support change. Our prisons are overpopulated, but the problems are deeper than mere overpopulation, which is just a result of the overly harsh sentences our justice system habitually hands down. We should not begin releasing people from prison merely to free up more room inside our institutions. But we should allow those who have worked toward changing their lives for the better in prison a chance to live life outside the prison walls. I urge our society to consider lighter sentences. When a person receives a life sentence without parole, that person is doomed to die in prison. He or she now has nothing to live for and no reason to change. Overly harsh sentences make prisons more dangerous for everyone. Visit a prison and talk to officers, counselors, teachers, and offenders. You will be surprised what you learn. It is about time we all start caring about these men and women, not just locking them up, forgetting about them, and deciding they are not our problem.

Reform Must Grow

As a teacher, I learned firsthand about the structure prison can offer. Once these offenders are off the streets and in the structured environment, they are able to learn about respect, education, team-work, and kindness, things that so many of us were blessed to have been taught by our parents. I believe a knowledge of the possible reform benefits prisons can offer—if we pursue it—is important for everyone.

Offenders do not remain the same people over the course of decades in prison. Inside, they can participate in many programs to change their lives, and I believe they deserve to put that change into action outside the walls.

Many inmates have grown up in prison, and they just walk the same daily routine, day after day, not making efforts toward change. But many of the men I met and with whom I worked have shown me they have changed. They do admit they committed a crime, sometimes even taking a life, yet they feel remorse, and if put back on the streets, they know they wouldn't do it again. They have been given the tools they need. They have learned how to work with others, to manage anger, and to handle emotions. While I know many would not accept their words on faith, working in a prison, you have the opportunity to see the actions of inmates who have undergone a powerful transformation. Reform can take years, but if we as a nation do not support it in prisons and follow through on opportunities outside the walls, the futures of thousands of men and women who could once again contribute to free society will dissolve.

I believe that everyone leaving prison needs, at a minimum, a high school diploma or GED. Without these tools, released offenders will fail on the outside. They need to learn about respect, work ethic, kindness, selflessness, opportunity. And they need to be reminded how life isn't fair. In short, they need to learn what was denied them when they were growing up.

Yet educational reform in the justice system needs to include so much more. As I remember the students with whom I worked in school, I think about how they can continue to educate themselves while still helping others. Those with life sentences who have been in prison for ten years or more still need to find value in life. Psychiatrists, counselors, officers, teachers, and others who work with prison inmates on a daily basis have a pretty good idea of which ones could possibly make it on the outside.

We need a program to test the skills inmates are truly capable of mastering. I propose that, as part of an educational program, those offenders with life sentences who have already served at least ten years and are making noteworthy progress be given jobs as mentors to new inmates. Let the teachers, guards, and other professionals really see what they can do.

Each eligible offender would be assigned a new inmate with whom to work, regardless of race, language barriers, gang affiliation, and other factors an additional test of whether the mentors could put secondary considerations aside for the benefit of their mentees. Prison profes- sionals would evaluate the mentor's ability to help the new inmates adjust and thrive in prison life whether they could help their mentees' personal growth, assist them in staying away from gang life, gaining an education, and learning about work ethic and respect. The inmate- mentors would be expected to help their mentees study for school, help them work through anger issues, and walk them through family deaths or comparable disappointments. And, if the inmate-mentors show ability and competence in rehabilitating others, their life sentences could perhaps be reconsidered.

If lifers were told that someday, if they worked hard and showed positive change, they might earn a right to receive a second chance on the outside, rehabilitation could improve in prisons. I have seen the impact that programs like this can have firsthand. I have seen gang leaders step down and take on new, positive authority.

Rehabilitation should be available to everyone. Everyone should have the chance to show he or she can change. Not everyone is capable of living in society outside of prison walls, but we should evaluate those who pursue education, stay out of trouble, and take on the well being of others as a personal challenge to see if they may be. Perhaps the possibility of parole could be reviewed after offenders have worked five or ten years as a rehabilitation mentor, depending on the amount of time they have already served. These people now would have something to live for, and perhaps, knowing this, they would be motivated to stay out of trouble.

I believe that when offenders see lifers given a second chance, when they see someone who was originally sentenced to die in prison walk out of there, some will be changed by it. I strongly believe we need to come together with politicians and correctional staff to help make this change happen. Let's be the better people and rise above all the negativity and help inmates, who, when you boil it down, are still just people who weren't given a chance at life from birth on—people who grew up dodging bullets, looking for their next meal, and living with people who exposed them to things their young minds didn't understand. Let's educate them so when they exit prison, they leave as different people.

In the countries where life sentences are limited to fifteen to twenty-five years, many of the men and women who exit prison don't reenter. They have been changed and are now people who understand work ethic, accountability, collaboration, patience, kindness, sorrow, and how to deal with emotions. Educational reform can and will make a difference if we get on board and want change in this world.

In England and Wales, a life sentence is considered served and an offender becomes eligible for parole or early release after serving an average of fifteen years. In France, inmates jailed for life are eligible after serving eighteen years or, for a repeat offence, twenty-two years. In Germany, after fifteen years, lifers are able to apply for parole. Denmark allows a pardoning hearing after twelve years, and in Poland, twenty-five years is considered a life sentence. But in the United States, a life sentence means you are sentenced to die in prison.

No good reform can come of such a sentence. If we continue to leave someone in prison for life, what does life mean to them? What value does it hold? There is little incentive to stop committing crimes, even inside the prison walls. In my work inside the Walls, I learned how many inmates cause trouble simply out of boredom, just to change up the monotony. Our society, our country, can do better than this!

My last day in prison work was August 11, 2017. My heart still aches with the sadness that so many of my inmate students encountered in their lives. I cry for the teenagers who slipped through the cracks, making poor decisions and now paying for those decisions for the rest of their lives. Who's at fault? A child who learns from their environment or the environment? There are too many children in the bodies of men and women simply existing in our prison systems, denied the education and nurturing they need to mature and truly live.

Join the reform movement—for justice, for education. Consider the perspective of my former students and the thousands across the nation just like them. Join the movement to educate them to see their true potential, allowing them to learn, not just about work ethic and accountability, and then allowing them to use their skills in the free air. Let them exit prison with a different perspective on life: a chance to live.

The world in which these offenders live is not a world I ever knew about or, in all honesty, ever thought about. The offenders changed my thought process and gave me an experience I will never forget. I want to see these men have the opportunity to work real jobs that make them proud, to have families they can come home to every night. We can't just forget about them. It is sad that our society did not help these offenders before they ended up in prison, but I believe it is not too late, and it is our duty to fix this problem. We need to keep others from going to prison, and we need to give back to those sitting in prison now. We all need to take accountability.

Even those of you who believe in the toughness of our current justice system should consider the tax benefits of reform. Offenders in prison are now working every day, given a warm bed, three meals a day, recreation, libraries, barbers, medical assistance, and more on the taxpayer's dime. Wouldn't it make more sense and benefit us all if they learned the necessary skills in prison so that they could then go out in the world and succeed on their own, paying their own way?

What does life mean to you? Do you truly believe in your heart that no one can change and that no one who committed a crime deserves a second chance? If that is how you feel, I invite you to visit a prison, detention center, or jail. Talk to people whom you never conversed with in the past and I assure you, it will open your eyes as it did mine when I walked through those seven doors each day. There are lives that can be saved behind those doors. I am hopeful that their stories will encourage more people to accept the challenge of being prison workers and teachers. Justice reform is coming to the forefront of political discussion. We can make a difference!

I am not a politician. I have made no great study of the statistics on recidivism (the tendency of a convicted criminal to reoffend). My perspective on this issue is purely that of an educator and someone who has been inside the Walls and seen. I know what I have witnessed firsthand. I saw what my students accomplished and how they transformed. They worked together, allowed themselves to be vulnerable for the benefit of others, and they became a team, creating a safe environment that allowed even more growth and change to occur. I know education works, and I am convinced that more needs to be done. More classes and opportunities need to be offered, so more life-changing transformations can occur. Most of these men will never know that I continue to check on them and ask others how they are doing. I sincerely hope they get a chance to read this book. I want them to know how much I believe in them.

Even though I am no longer teaching in their prison, I hope they take what they have learned in the classroom and continue to apply it to their lives. I hope they keep paying it forward. I hope they still hear my voice telling them I won't feel sorry for them. They have to take the initiative to work hard in order to make a difference. Life isn't fair, but it goes on. I hope they hear me telling them to "Eat, Sleep, Math." It doesn't apply only in the classroom. It is a metaphor they can use for everything that happens in their lives.

Although a change in circumstances caused me to leave my teaching position after three years of prison work, my passion for prison educational reform has only grown. I am excited about all that is being done. Other educators echo my thoughts that our job is not to continue to punish these offenders but instead to be there to educate and to help rehabilitate offenders so that new men and women can reenter society one day. The changes happening in the courts and in our political system are the beginning steps we desperately need to take in order to walk more steadily toward reform, but they are not enough. I will continue to tell my story, continue to share the stories of my tutors and my students, and continue to be the voice of change that I promised those men the day we parted at Door Seven.

About the Author

As the youngest of five children raised in the Upper Peninsula of Michigan, Beth Rondeau grew up in an environment where putting hard work and education first was expected. She put that work ethic to good use professionally, earning her bachelor of science degree in mathematics with a minor in all sciences and teaching endorsement from Michigan Technological University and her master of arts degree in supervision and instruction from Northern Michigan University.

Beth embarked on a prestigious educational career, teaching math and science at schools with graduating class sizes from 14 to 180 and students spanning a wide range of ages. For Beth, teaching doesn't just begin and end in the classroom. What is learnt within the walls of a classroom transcends to all areas of a student's life. It is important to her to instill in her students a good work ethic, how to be a valued team member, the importance of accountability and strong leadership, and the value of risk taking and learning from one's mistakes. In 2018, Beth received Iowa's Sanford Teacher Award, an award given annually to one inspirational teacher in each state.

For three years, Beth taught offenders in a maximum-security penitentiary. In 2017, Beth was named Iowa's Correctional Teacher of the Year. She has presented on mathematics at multiple conferences for educators of adults, including the WIOA Partners Conference. Additionally, she has presented internationally, coaching educators through her life-changing experiences about taking every opportunity to connect with students. As the owner of the 7th Door LLC, Beth coaches kids to thrive in high school and beyond.